The MicroWave DIABETES COOKBOOK

By Betty Marks

SURREY BOOKS
230 East Ohio Street
Suite 120
Chicago, Illinois 60611

THE MICROWAVE DIABETES COOKBOOK is published by Surrey Books, Inc., 230 E. Ohio St., Suite 120, Chicago, Illinois 60611

This book is manufactured in the United States of America.

First edition: 4 5

Library of Congress Cataloging-in-Publication Data:

Marks, Betty.
   The microwave diabetes cookbook / Betty Marks.
      216 p.   cm.
   Includes index.
   ISBN 0-940625-26-1
      1. Diabetes–Diet therapy–Recipes. 2. Microwave cookery.
   I. Title.
   RC662.M354 1991
   641.5' 6314–dc20   90-24555
                                                              CIP

Editorial production: *Bookcrafters, Inc., Chicago*
Cover design and art direction: *Hughes & Co., Chicago*
Illustrations: *Elizabeth Allen*

Single copies may be ordered by sending check or money order for cover price of book plus $2.50 per book for shipping and handling to Surrey Books at the above address. The Surrey Books catalog is also available from the publisher free of charge.

This title is distributed to the trade by Publishers Group West.

For two dear friends—

Jane Brody, whose good food inspires me,
and Fran Korein, who taught me the magic of microwaves.

Acknowledgments

Testing and tasting new foods is always an experience—sometimes agreeable, other times not so great. My warm thanks for doing this go to two of my favorite cooks, Nancy Henderson and Nancy Racusin.

My gratitude is also extended to the many friends and neighbors who willingly ate my dishes, mostly with glee, often with lucid commentary. These include Cindy and Jeff Brody, Jane Brody and Richard Engquist, Fran Korein and Ray Belsky, Helen and Norman Stern, Eleanor and Marc Anderson, and Bernice and Earl Balis.

I am especially grateful to Dr. Daniel Lorber of the Diabetes Control Foundation for his introductory remarks, and to the indispensable Hope Warshaw, M.M.Sc., R.D., for her careful and accurate nutritional analyses.

Contents

Preface

When I was remodeling my kitchen, my good friend Fran Korein asked if a microwave were in the plans. I was hesitant about this new appliance, not wanting to learn about all those push-buttons and timing devices. But a few of Fran's delicious meals prepared in no time at all convinced me that the microwave was the twentieth century's boon to busy people. I could spend the day doing my work or hiking in the mountains, skiing, running, swimming, or enjoying ballroom dancing and get back to the house to prepare a healthful meal in no time at all.

So I installed a microwave oven, and as I progressed with my experimenting, it occurred to me that the kind of heart-healthy cooking that I did could be shared with others who have diabetes or need to watch their food intake carefully for other reasons. I learned that the microwave cooked without fat, made vegetables that did not lose their vigor in a pot of water, and even allowed me to bake delicious breads, muffins, and cakes. Foods cooked in the microwave retain their nutrients and stay hotter longer.

In addition to cutting down cooking time radically, using the microwave eliminates the need to scrub pots since food can be cooked *on* the very dish on which it will be served. Less time is needed in planning and preparing meals, leaving one free to pursue whatever activities take precedence over kitchen duty, whether it's work or pleasure. Children usually can learn to use the microwave safely and easily, and one's urge for a snack or meal can be satisfied in minutes.

It is my hope that by using these fast but good recipes, my readers will enjoy well balanced, tasty, and attractive meals in minutes and spend the time saved in pursuits that bring them joy and contentment.

Betty Marks
New York City
November, 1990

Foreword

People with diabetes have a primary concern in their daily lives. Staying in good control requires constant vigilance in many aspects of every day's chores and pleasures. Eating at regular times, and sometimes in between, exercising, and balancing insulin intake with energy expenditure is a full-time task.

Good nutrition is another major concern for those who want to keep trim and stay as healthy as possible even though they lead busy lives. Very often, food is needed in a hurry. Betty Marks, who fills her life with many activities, addresses this dilemma in this, her fourth, cookbook. The microwave has proved a boon to her in the preparation of more than one hundred healthful recipes.

As a person whose life depends upon several daily doses of insulin, Betty has developed a way to make many marvelous meals! And in her *Microwave Diabetes Cookbook* she shares these fast and simple methods with all of you whose needs are as demanding as her own.

All too often in the past, family and friends have not wanted to eat the same food that the family member with diabetes has selected. But we now know that everyone can benefit from a healthy-heart diet—one that is low in fat, cholesterol, and sodium, is moderate in calories, and does not contain the empty calories of sugar and honey.

The recipes chosen for inclusion in *The Microwave Diabetes Cookbook* range from appetizers, soups, fish, meat and poultry, grains and vegetables, pastas, sauces, baked breads and muffins to desserts. They are all simple to prepare and fast to cook. Everyone can enjoy the good taste and speed of these recipes that satisfy the appetite *and* the need to eat correctly.

With this book's culinary contributions, the management of diabetes mellitus becomes more agreeable and, because of the vast time saving, an opportunity to lead a more enjoyable and richer life.

Daniel Louis Lorber, M.D., F.A.C.P.
Associate Clinical Professor of Medicine,
Albert Einstein College of Medicine, Bronx, NY,
and Medical Director, Diabetes Control Foundation,
Flushing, New York

Introduction

A quick, easy, tasty recipe repertory for people with diabetes? Sounds impossible! Yet once again Betty Marks has created such a collection of recipes, chock full of interesting food combinations and unique ingredient mixtures. These recipes will help turn the rigor of daily meal planning into an interesting adventure with food. Best yet, these recipes are quick and easy because they're all microwavable. Thus, they go hand-in-hand with today's fast-paced lifestyle.

"Dull," "boring," "repetitive," "lacks zip"—as a registered dietitian, these are words I often hear to describe eating on a diabetes meal plan. Unfortunately, this perspective leads many people to stray off plan. To maximize adherence to a diabetes meal plan—and thus to improve management of diabetes—it's essential to master the art of integrating both taste and zip into daily food preparation.

Today's recommendations for diabetes nutrition management, simply stated, are simply a call for healthy eating. The same dietary guidelines steering diabetes meal planning are those touted loud and clear for all Americans: eat less fat, saturated fat, and cholesterol, more starches and fiber, limited sweets, and less protein. These goals are rigorously kept in focus in *The Microwave Diabetes Cookbook*.

To further guide the meal-maker in this quest for sound nutrition, each recipe includes nutritional data, stating per-serving total calories and amounts of dietary fiber, sodium, cholesterol, carbohydrates, protein, and fat—saturated, polyunsaturated, and monounsaturated. These values were derived using the computer program "Recipe Analysis and Exchange List Conversion" developed by Lawrence Wheeler, M.D., Ph.D., and Madelyn Wheeler, M.S., R.D., C.D.E. Nutrition information in this program relies mainly on United States Department of Agriculture figures.

Along with the nutritional evaluation, each recipe also provides food exchange calculations. The exchange system, developed by The American Dietetic Association and The American Diabetes Association, assists people with diabetes in meal planning. The food exchanges provided here were determined according to recommended guidelines of The American Diabetes Association.

To sum up, Betty Marks proves once again in this cookbook that diabetes management, healthy eating, fast and easy preparation, and tasty meals can harmoniously coexist on the same dinner plate.

Hope S. Warshaw, M.M.Sc., R.D., C.D.E.
Nutrition Consultant, Boston, Massachusetts

Measures and Equivalents

METRIC CONVERSIONS, FLUID

United States	Metric
4¼ cups, or 1 quart plus 2 ounces	= 1 liter
2⅛ cups, or 1 pint plus 1 ounce	= ½ liter
¼ teaspoon	= 1.25 milliliters
½ teaspoon	= 2.5 milliliters
1 teaspoon	= 5 milliliters
1 tablespoon	= 15 milliliters
¼ cup	= 63 milliliters
⅓ cup	= 84 milliliters
½ cup	= 125 milliliters
1 cup	= ¼ liter or 250 milliliters
1 pint	= .473 liter
1 quart	= .946 liter

METRIC CONVERSIONS, DRY

United States	Metric
.035 ounce	= 1 gram
1 ounce	= 28.35 grams
3.5 ounces	= 100 grams
4 ounces	= 114 grams
8 ounces (1 cup)	= 226.78 grams
1 pound	= 454 grams
1 pound, 1.5 ounces	= 500 grams
2.21 pounds	= 1 kilogram

U.S. EQUIVALENT MEASUREMENTS

1 tablespoon = 3 teaspoons
¼ cup = 4 tablespoons
⅓ cup = 5⅓ tablespoons
½ cup = 8 tablespoons
¾ cup = 12 tablespoons
1 cup = 16 tablespoons
1 pint = 2 cups
1 quart = 4 cups
1 gallon = 4 quarts
1 pound = 16 ounces

Note: Measurements of less than ⅛ of a teaspoon are called a "dash" or a "pinch."

METRIC EQUIVALENT MEASUREMENTS

Fluid Measurements

1 deciliter = 0.1 (1/10) liter
1 milliliter = 0.001 (1/1000) liter

Weight Measurements

kilogram = 1,000 grams (slightly more than 2 pounds, or about 2.2 pounds)
gram = 0.001 (1/1000) kilogram
milligram = 0.001 (1/1000) gram

NUTRITIONAL ABBREVIATIONS

Chol = cholesterol
Carbo = carbohydrates
Prot = protein
Na = sodium, or salt

Sat = saturated
Poly = polyunsaturated
Mono = monounsaturated
g = grams
mg = milligrams

Microwave Hints

How to Use the Microwave

- Consult manufacturer's instructions and learn the wattage of your microwave.

- Most microwave recipes, including those in this book, are developed for 600–700-watt ovens. If your oven is smaller than 600 watts, adjust the cooking times as follows:

  - 500 to 600 watts: add 15 seconds to every minute of cooking time specified.

  - 400 to 500 watts: add 30 seconds to every minute of cooking time specified in recipe.

  - If your oven is less than 500 watts, use "High" setting even when directions call for 50 percent power.

It is better to undercook food since it can always be returned to the oven for additional time. Check meat, poultry, fish, and vegetables for doneness by piercing with a fork.

The size of the microwave oven is relative to the wattage: the higher, the larger. If measuring containers suggested in recipes do not fit in your microwave, use smaller bowls, cups, etc., in multiples.

- For cooking muffins and breads at altitudes of 3,500 feet and above, use larger pans and fill only halfway. Use more liquid and cook longer than specified time. Elevate baking dish on inverted saucer.

- Power levels:
  - High—100%
  - Medium High—70%
  - Medium—50%
  - Medium Low or Defrost—30%
  - Low—10%

- If you are visually impaired, Braille overlays are available from microwave manufacturers.

- Use only microwave-safe plates or dishes. Any non-metal dish; glass or ceramic casserole; Pyrex measuring cup, pie plate, or loaf pan may be used. Round or oval dishes are the best for even cooking.

- Paper plates, towels, wax paper, and plastic wrap may be used in the microwave. Covering foods with wax paper or plastic wrap helps steam food while keeping it moist and preventing splattering.

- To vent plastic wrap, pierce with a knife or fold under one side. Do not use plastic wrap if cooking for long periods of time, and try not to let heated plastic wrap come in contact with food. When removing plastic wrap or wax paper from heated dishes, peel off away from you to avoid steam burns.

- Do not use recycled paper towels or bags.

- Use pot holders when removing dishes from the microwave.

- Do not use microwave with door open; most models will not operate with the door open.

- Before starting to cook, read the recipe through carefully and assemble all ingredients, placing them on kitchen counter in order of their use. To save more time, keep the larder stocked by reviewing meal plans for the week ahead and shopping for the required ingredients.

- Do not use plastic containers such as margarine or butter tubs in microwave, as they may melt at high temperatures.

- Aluminum foil may be used around edges of cooking dishes, but metal pans should not be used, and all metals should be kept away from sides of the oven.

- Learn about microwaves: microwaves are short radio waves that penetrate food, starting on the outer layer and moving inward gradually. They cause food molecules to move, producing friction. This makes heat that cooks food. Microwaves penetrate food from all directions, and the heating takes place in the food itself. No heat is produced in the oven, which keeps the kitchen cool. Microwaves do not change the chemical composition of food, they are not harmful, and there is no danger of radiation.

- To clean microwave oven: place a small bowl of water in microwave, and heat on High for 2 minutes or until water boils. Remove water and wipe clean.

- Microwave ovens are great time-savers, but they are an accessory. They are not appropriate for cooking all foods. They are not recommended for browning and crisping food nor for roasting chickens, turkey, or beef. The microwave is superb for cooking vegetables, fish, stews, soups, casseroles, chicken and turkey chunks, and quick breads and muffins. Since the microwave extracts one-third more fat from meat than a conventional oven while holding in other juices, it benefits people who want moist, low-fat foods.

Cooking Tips

- Standing Time: recipes often call for some additional cooking that takes place after dish is removed from the oven.

- Vegetables can be cooked in the microwave while another dish is "standing."

- Partially freeze meat or poultry (about 30 minutes) for easier slicing.

- Do not refreeze meats thawed in microwave, and do not partially cook food.

- Small pieces of meat and poultry cook faster than large chunks, thin portions faster than thick, and small quantities of food cook faster than large quantities. Deboned meat or poultry cooks faster and more evenly.

- Do not leave food in microwave for more than two hours.

- Stir foods in mid-cycle or several times for even cooking. Move undercooked food to outside of dish and those pieces that are done to the center.

- Rotate cooking dish in microwave oven unless your microwave is equipped with a turntable. Wind-up turntables may be purchased for use in the microwave oven.

- Turn large foods such as squash, eggplant, potatoes over in mid-cycle for even cooking.

- Arrange uniform meat or poultry pieces in a single layer or circle, leaving center empty.

- To get more juice from a lemon or orange, heat in microwave for half a minute or so before squeezing.

- Elevate cooking dishes when called for (as in some baked recipes) on an inverted saucer. This allows microwaves to circulate under dish and cook more evenly.

- To toast nuts and seeds, place on 9-inch glass pie plate and cook on High for 1 to 2 minutes, shaking dish once. Pine nuts (pignoli), sunflower or pumpkin seeds, and sesame seeds may be toasted this way. Cover with paper towels to avoid popping. Nuts such as walnuts, almonds, filberts, and pecans may be toasted the same way but without covering. Add a generous shake of cinnamon to the nuts for flavor.

Special Utensils

- In addition to 1- and 2-cup measures, larger microwave-safe measures are also recommended, and they are available in sizes from 1 to 5 quarts. Casseroles and baking dishes also come in these sizes.

- 8- to 9-inch glass and ceramic pie plates are very useful.

- For baking muffins, a plastic microwave-safe muffin tin is helpful. However, if this is difficult to find, I recommend using paper hot cups (unwaxed) cut down about halfway. They may then be filled partially with muffin mixture and baked in the microwave safely.

• Browning dishes are available, made by Corning and other manufacturers. Follow directions for first heating the dish. (Mine is heated with the oven on High for 5 minutes.) When the recipe calls for browning fish, chicken, or beef, place slices on the heated dish and return to the oven. Care should be taken when removing the dish from the oven, as it will be quite hot.

• Probes and thermometers are useful to determine doneness by temperature.

Appetizers

Many people enjoy sitting down with a few nibbles before having their main meal. Others like to graze as a style of eating—tasting a variety of small dishes rather than eating one large entree. Here are a variety of offerings, all of which are tasty and truly appetizing, that will satisfy either desire.

Blue Corn Crisps

16 blue corn tortilla chips
¼ cup low-fat mozzarella or cheese sub-
    stitute, shredded
2 tablespoons mild salsa

Line platter with wax paper and arrange tortilla
chips over it. Sprinkle grated cheese over each chip
and top with a dab of sauce. Microwave on High
just until cheese melts, about 1 minute. Serve while
warm.

- **Serves:** 4 (4 per serving)
- **Cooking time:** 1 minute
- **Preparation time:** 2 minutes
- **Per Serving:** 4 Chol (mg); 9 Carbo (g); 3 Prot (g);
    201 Na (mg)
    Dietary Fiber: 1.5 g
    Fat (g): 4; Sat 1.4; Poly 1.3; Mono .8
    Calories: 78
    Exchanges: ½ starch/bread; 1 fat

Clam Dip

¼ cup low-fat cottage cheese
¼ cup Yogurt Sour Cream (see index)
1 6½-ounce can minced clams, drained
1 tablespoons shallots, minced
1 teaspoon horseradish
Dash tabasco sauce or cayenne pepper

Whip cottage cheese and yogurt sour cream in blender until smooth. Add remaining ingredients, blend, and place in 2-cup microwave-safe measure. Microwave on Medium (50%) 1 minute, stirring once. Serve warm or chilled with blue corn chips or crudités.

· **Serves:** 8 (2-tablespoon servings)
· **Cooking time:** 1 minute
· **Preparation time:** 5 minutes
· **Per Serving:** 16 Chol (mg); 2 Carbo (g); 7 Prot (g);
      56 Na (mg)
   Dietary Fiber: 0
   Fat (g): 1; Sat .1; Poly .1; Mono .1
   Calories: 44
   Exchanges: 1 lean meat

   Calculation does not include chips or vegetables.

Hot Bean Dip

1 8-ounce can of kidney or pinto beans,
    rinsed and drained
2 cloves garlic, minced
¼ cup shallots, chopped
½ cup tofu (bean curd)
1 medium stalk celery, chopped
2 tablespoons mild salsa
2 tablespoons part-skim mozzarella
    cheese, grated
Parsley, chopped, for garnish

Mix all ingredients except last two in blender or
food processor and puree. Place in 16-ounce microwave glass bowl, and microwave on High for 1 minute. Remove, stir to mix, sprinkle with cheese, and
return to microwave on High for another 40 seconds, just until cheese melts. Garnish with sprinkle
of chopped parsley. Serve as dip with vegetable
crudités.

· **Serves:** 4 (2-tablespoon servings)
· **Cooking time:** 2 minutes
· **Preparation time:** 5 minutes
· **Per Serving:** 5 Chol (mg);   13 Carbo (g);   8 Prot (g);
    373 Na (mg)
    Dietary Fiber: 2.7 g
    Fat (g):   3;   Sat 1.1;   Poly .9;   Mono .7
    Calories: 109
    Exchanges: 1 starch/bread;   ½ lean meat

Pepper Pizza

4 6-inch corn tortillas
1 teaspoon olive oil
2 cloves garlic, minced
½ medium green bell pepper, julienned
½ medium red bell pepper, julienned
½ cup fresh mushrooms, sliced
¼ cup tomato puree
Oregano
2 tablespoons part-skim mozzarella (or no-fat cheese substitute), grated

Place tortillas in oven and microwave on High for 3 minutes until crisp. Remove from oven and set aside. Place olive oil in small glass bowl with garlic and peppers. Microwave on High for 2 minutes.

Mix in tomato puree, oregano, and sliced mushrooms, and microwave for 1½ minutes more. Spread on top of tortillas, and sprinkle with cheese. Place tortillas on serving dish and microwave for 30 to 40 seconds until cheese melts.

· **Serves:** 4
· **Cooking time:** 7 minutes
· **Preparation time:** 10 minutes
· **Per Serving:** 5 Chol (mg); 17 Carbo (g); 5 Prot (g); 158 Na (mg)
   Dietary Fiber: 1.8 g
   Fat (g): 4; Sat 1.1; Poly .2; Mono 1.2
   Calories: 115
   Exchanges: ½ starch/bread; 1 vegetable; 1 fat

Potato Cheese Chips

2 medium Idaho potatoes, about 1
    pound
2 ounces low-fat shredded cheese—
    Alpine Lace, part skim mozzarella,
    etc.
¼ teaspoon each of garlic powder, chili
    powder, and dried basil
Dash of pepper to taste

Wash potatoes and prick each with a fork. Wrap
each potato in microwave-safe paper towel and
place end-to-end in oven. Microwave on High for 4
to 5 minutes. Turn potatoes over and microwave on
High another 4 to 5 minutes. Unwrap, let cool, and
refrigerate.

When chilled, cut into ¼-inch slices and top
with sprinkling of cheese, a dusting of combined
spices, and dash of pepper.

Line oven with paper towels and arrange potato
slices on them. Microwave for 30 to 40 seconds, just
until cheese melts. Makes 16 slices.

- **Serves:** 4 (4 slices per serving)
- **Cooking time:** 8½ to 10½ minutes
- **Preparation time:** 5 minutes plus chilling time
- **Per Serving:** 8 Chol (mg); 13 Carbo (g); 5 Prot (g);
    72 Na (mg)
    Dietary Fiber: 1.8 g
    Fat (g) 2; Sat 1.5; Poly .1; Mono .6;
    Calories: 91
    Exchanges: 1 starch/bread

Soup

Soup is a splendid way to start a meal, or indeed be a major part of the meal itself. The soups in this section are simple to prepare and with the microwave and food processor take but minutes to cook. Many use fresh vegetables, some use nutritious beans, and the addition of non-fat milk or yogurt adds an extra bit of calcium. Spices, seasonings, and garnishes provide appealing tastes and colors. Chopped parsley, paprika, diced bell peppers, or shredded carrots lend texture as a topping, too.

When transferring hot liquid to the blender or processor, use only small amounts at a time and let cool a little before blending. The pureed soup can always be returned to the microwave oven for rewarming.

Cauliflower Soup

1 pound cauliflower, trimmed, cut into florets
1 medium carrot, scraped and diced
1 stalk celery with leaves, sliced
½ onion, sliced
1 teaspoon Vogue chicken-base flavor mixed with ½ cup water
2 cups water
¼ cup non-fat dry milk
1 teaspoon curry powder
1 teaspoon caraway seeds
½ teaspoon red pepper flakes
Salt and pepper to taste
Juice of ½ lemon
Parsley for garnish
Dash paprika

Place cauliflower, carrot, celery, onion, and water and flavoring in a 2-quart measure. Microwave on High for 8 minutes, stirring once, until cauliflower stems are soft. Let cool a few minutes, and place in blender or food processor with 2 cups of water (as needed to thin) and puree. Add milk and curry powder and process for a few seconds.

Return to measure, stir in caraway seeds, red pepper flakes, and salt and pepper to taste. Microwave about 2 to 3 minutes to warm. Stir in lemon juice, and garnish with parsley and dash of paprika.

· **Serves:** 4
· **Cooking time:** 10 to 11 minutes
· **Preparation time:** 10 minutes
· **Per Serving:** 1 Chol (mg); 11 Carbo (g); 4 Prot (g);
     75 Na (mg)
     Dietary Fiber: 3.5 g
     Fat (g): 0; Sat .1; Poly .2; Mono .1
     Calories: 57
     Exchanges: 2 vegetable

Chicken Broth

1 broiler chicken, cut up, or 2 pounds
  chicken parts
4 cloves garlic
2 stalks celery with tops, chopped
  coarsely
6 parsley sprigs
1 bay leaf
6 peppercorns
2 medium onions, quartered
2 carrots, cut in half
1 parsnip, cut in half
3 quarts water

Place all ingredients in a 5-quart measure or casserole and cover with vented plastic wrap. Microwave on High for 15 minutes. Skim off any foam that accumulates. Recover and microwave on 50% for 15 minutes, still skimming off any froth.

Strain stock into a bowl and let rest to room temperature. Discard solids, or give the cooked chicken meat to the cat. Cool stock in refrigerator, and discard fat that congeals on surface. Place stock in small containers and freeze for future use. Makes 3 quarts.

· **Serves:** 12 (1-cup servings)
· **Cooking time:** 30 minutes
· **Preparation time:** 10 minutes
· **Per Serving:** 0 Chol (mg);   4 Carbo (g);   1 Prot (g);
     10 Na (mg)
     Dietary Fiber: 0
     Fat (g):   0;   Sat 0;   Poly 0;   Mono 0
     Calories: 20
     Exchanges: Free

Creamy Carrot Soup

2 teaspoons canola oil
1 teaspoon whole wheat flour
2 cups carrots, scraped and sliced
2 cups Chicken Broth (see previous recipe)
Pinch salt
¼ teaspoon dried thyme
1 bay leaf
½ teaspoon fresh ginger root, chopped
2 teaspoons frozen orange juice concentrate
¼ teaspoon dried tarragon
Fresh pepper to taste
1 cup skim milk
¼ cup non-fat dry milk
Few sprigs fresh mint or ½ teaspoon dried mint; or fresh parsley for garnish

Mix first 8 ingredients in a 2-quart measure. Microwave for 10 minutes on High. Let cool a few minutes. Discard bay leaf and turn into food processor or blender a little at a time. Process to blend.

(Please turn page)

Add orange juice, tarragon, pepper, and milk and blend. Return to original container and microwave on High for 1 to 2 minutes until warmed through. Top with garnish of mint or parsley. May also be served chilled.

· **Serves:** 4
· **Cooking time:** 11 to 12 minutes
· **Preparation time:** 10 minutes
· **Per Serving:** 2 Chol (mg);   15 Carbo (g);   5 Prot (g);   109 Na (mg)
    Dietary Fiber: 1.9g
    Fat (g):   2;   Sat .4;   Poly .2;   Mono 1.6
    Calories: 97
    Exchanges: 2 vegetable; ½ skim milk

Crunchy Vegetable Soup

1½ cups asparagus, about 6 spears
1 medium carrot, chopped fine
1 stalk celery, chopped fine
2 tablespoons onion, chopped
2 medium mushrooms, sliced
1 cup Chicken Broth (see index)
1 cup non-fat plain yogurt
Dash tarragon
Dash cayenne
Pepper to taste
Diced pimentos for garnish

Place asparagus spears on dish with a little water and cover with wax paper. Microwave on High for 5 to 6 minutes. Cut into 1-inch pieces and place in food processor with vegetables and chicken broth. Process until mixed.

Turn into 8-cup measure and microwave on High for 6 to 8 minutes until soup simmers. Stir in yogurt. Serve with dusting of tarragon, cayenne, and pepper and a garnish of diced pimentos.

(Please turn page)

May be served warm or chilled. Any combination of vegetables may be used for this potage—broccoli, cauliflower, cucumbers, radishes—just as long as they are crunchable.

· **Serves:** 4
· **Cooking time:** 11 to 14 minutes
· **Preparation time:** 10 minutes
· **Per Serving:** 2 Chol (mg);   9 Carbo (g);   5 Prot (g);
      63 Na (mg)
      Dietary Fiber: 2.5g
      Fat (g):   1;   Sat .4;   Poly .3;   Mono .2
      Calories: 55
      Exchanges: 2 vegetable

Egg Drop Soup

4 cups Chicken Broth (see index)
¼ cup scallions sliced
½ cup frozen peas and mushrooms
1 tablespoon fresh gingeroot, minced
   fine
2 teaspoons low-sodium soy sauce
2 eggs, one yolk only, well beaten

Pour the stock into a 6-cup casserole or measure and cover with vented plastic wrap. Microwave on High for 8 to 10 minutes, until stock boils. Add scallions, peas and mushrooms, gingeroot, and soy sauce. Microwave on High another 1 minute. Uncover and slowly drizzle egg into the soup, using a circular motion.

· **Serves:** 4
· **Cooking time:** 9 to 11 minutes
· **Preparation time:** 5 minutes
· **Per Serving:** 70 Chol (mg);   6 Carbo (g);   4 Prot (g);
      141 Na (mg)
   Dietary Fiber: 1.0g
   Fat (g):   2; Sat .5; Poly .3; Mono .6
   Calories: 43
   Exchanges: 1 vegetable

Garden Green Soup

1 teaspoon canola oil
4 shallots, sliced
3 cloves garlic, minced
4 cups mixed greens, rinsed well and
  shredded (use combination of romaine
  and red leaf or Boston lettuce, spinach, escarole, and sorrel)
2 cups skim milk
1 cup Chicken Broth (see index)
1 tablespoon oat bran
¼ cup fresh basil, chopped, (or 1 teaspoon dried)
Rind of 1 lemon, grated
Pepper to taste

Place oil, shallots, and garlic in 2-quart measure, and microwave on High for 2 minutes. Add greens and stir to combine. Microwave on High for 2 to 3 minutes, stirring, until greens are wilted. Add remaining ingredients and transfer to a food processor, two cups at a time. Return to original container and microwave another 2 to 3 minutes to warm. Serve warm or chilled.

· Serves: 4
· Cooking time: 6 to 8 minutes
· Preparation time: 15 minutes
· Per Serving: 2 Chol (mg);   11 Carbo (g);   6 Prot (g);
    92 Na (mg)
  Dietary Fiber: 2.4g
  Fat (g): 1; Sat .3; Poly .2; Mono .8;
  Calories: 79
  Exchanges: 1 vegetable; ½ milk

Mexican Corn Soup

. . . .

1 carrot, shredded (about ½ cup)
1 medium green pepper, chopped (½ cup)
¼ cup shallots, chopped
1 teaspoon vegetable oil
1 cup corn niblets (fresh, canned, or frozen (thawed)
2 cups Chicken Broth (see index)
½ cup non-fat dry milk mixed with enough water to make 1 cup
⅛ teaspoon red pepper flakes
¼ teaspoon celery seed

Place carrot, green pepper, and shallots in a 2-quart casserole or measure with the vegetable oil, and microwave on High for 3 minutes. Add remaining ingredients, and transfer and mix in a food processor or blender, a little at a time. Return to original container and microwave on High 2 to 3 minutes until warm, stirring once.

· **Serves:** 4
· **Cooking time:** 5 to 6 minutes
· **Preparation time:** 10 minutes
· **Per Serving:** 3 Chol (mg); 19 Carbo (g); 5 Prot (g); 65 Na (mg)
   Dietary Fiber: 2.5g
   Fat (g): 0; Sat 0; Poly 0; Mono 0
   Calories: 91
   Exchanges: 1 starch/bread; ½ milk

Snow Pea Soup

4 cups Chicken Broth (see index)
¼ cup scallions, minced
¼ cup carrots, finely chopped
1 clove garlic, minced
1 teaspoon fresh ginger root, grated
1 teaspoon low-sodium soy sauce
¼ cup mushrooms, sliced
1 cup snow peas (about ¼ pound),
    washed and trimmed
4 ounces firm tofu (bean curd) cut into
    ½-inch cubes
Scallions, additional, for garnish

Place broth, scallions, carrots, garlic, ginger root, and soy sauce in an 8-cup measure. Microwave on High for 8 to 10 minutes. Add mushrooms and cook 5 minutes more on High. Add snow peas and microwave for 1 minute more on High. Stir in tofu and garnish with scallions.

· Serves: 4
· Cooking time: 14 to 16 minutes
· Preparation time: 15 minutes
· Per Serving: 0 Chol (mg);   8 Carbo (g);   4 Prot (g);
       61 Na (mg)
    Dietary Fiber: 1.3g
    Fat (g):   2;   Sat .2;   Poly .8;   Mono .3
    Calories: 39
    Exchanges: 1½ vegetable

Squash Soup

2 acorn or butternut squash, about 1
  pound each
½ cup onion, chopped
2 cups Chicken Broth (see index)
½ teaspoon cinnamon, ground
¼ teaspoon coriander, ground
¼ teaspoon cumin, ground
⅛ teaspoon turmeric
Fresh pepper to taste
1 tablespoon apple cider vinegar
1 cup buttermilk
4 tablespoons non-fat dry milk
1 tablespoon low-sodium soy sauce
1 tablespoon fresh parsley, chopped

Place whole squash in oven and microwave on High
for 2 minutes. Pierce deeply several times with a
fork. Microwave on High for 6 to 8 minutes more
until soft, turning squash over and rotating twice.
Let stand 5 minutes or until cool enough to handle.
Slice squash in half, discard seeds, and scrape out
pulp. There should be about 3 cups of pulp.

(Please turn page)

Let squash cool for 10 minutes; then turn into a blender or food processor with the onion and chicken stock and puree. Transfer to an 8-cup measuring bowl and add spices, vinegar, milks, and soy sauce. Microwave for 2 to 3 minutes until soup simmers. Adjust seasoning and serve with a garnish of parsley.

- **Serves:** 6 (1-cup servings)
- **Cooking time:** 13 minutes
- **Preparation time:** 10 to 13 minutes plus 15 minutes resting time
- **Per Serving:** 2 Chol (mg);   30 Carbo (g);   4 Prot (g);   168 Na (mg)
    Dietary Fiber: 5.1g
    Fat (g): 1; Sat .3; Poly .1; Mono .1
    Calories: 95
    Exchanges: 1½ starch/bread; ½ milk

Tomato Vegetable Soup

3 cups canned Italian plum tomatoes
1 tablespoon frozen apple juice
   concentrate
1 tablespoon scallions, minced (reserve
   green tops for garnish)
2 whole cloves
1 bay leaf
½ cup frozen peas, thawed
½ cup corn kernels (canned or, if frozen,
   thawed)
Dash pepper

Puree tomatoes in blender or food processor, and turn into a 9-inch-deep glass bowl or soup tureen. Add apple juice, scallions, cloves, and bay leaf and cover with vented plastic wrap. Microwave on High for 2 minutes.

Remove plastic, stir, and add peas and corn. Cover and microwave on High for 3 to 4 minutes more until heated through. Remove bay leaf and cloves, stir, and garnish with remaining green scallions and dashes of pepper.

· Serves: 4
· **Cooking time:** 5 to 6 minutes
· **Preparation time:** 5 minutes
· **Per Serving:** 0 Chol (mg) 16; Carbo (g) 3; Prot (g);
      312 Na (mg)
      Dietary Fiber: 3.6g
      Fat (g): 1; Sat .1; Poly .2; Mono .1
      Calories: 75
      Exchanges: 1 starch/bread

Vichyssoise

1 cup Chicken Broth (see index)
1 cup potatoes, peeled and cubed
1½ cups leeks, well washed, chopped
2 cups skim milk
Few dashes celery seed
¼ teaspoon salt
Dash fresh pepper
1 tablespoon part-skim ricotta cheese
Few dashes cayenne

Place broth, potatoes, and leeks in a food processor and blend to liquefy. Turn into a 2-quart measure, and microwave 3 to 5 minutes until vegetables are tender. Place remaining ingredients in food processor, add cooked vegetables, and process again until smooth. Pour into a bowl and chill before serving. Top with dusting of cayenne.

As a variation, this may also be made with sweet potatoes.

· Serves: 4
· Cooking time: 3 to 5 minutes
· Preparation time: 12 minutes
· Per Serving: 4 Chol (mg);   16 Carbo (g);   9 Prot (g);
      187 Na (mg)
    Dietary Fiber: 1.3g
    Fat (g):   1;   Sat .5;   Poly .3;   Mono .4
    Calories: 111
    Exchanges: ½ skim milk;   ½ starch/bread

White Bean Soup

2 cups celery, chopped
3 scallions, chopped
3 cloves garlic, chopped
1 teaspoon canola oil
1 medium onion, chopped
2 15-ounce cans Cannellini beans,
    drained, rinsed
2 tablespoons oat bran
3 allspice berries
1 cup Chicken Broth (see index)
1 cup water
Dash thyme
Dash cayenne
½ teaspoon dill weed
Juice of 1 lemon
Pepper to taste
Few sprigs fresh parsley for garnish

Place celery, scallions, garlic, oil, and onion in a 2-quart measure, and microwave on High for 3 minutes, stirring once. Add remaining ingredients except parsley, and microwave on High for 10 to 12

(Please turn page)

minutes more. Let cool a little and turn into food processor in small batches to puree. Return to microwave for 1 minute on High if necessary to re-warm. Garnish with parsley, and serve warm or chilled.

· Serves: 6
· **Cooking time:** 14 to 16 minutes
· **Preparation time:** 20 minutes
· **Per Serving:** 0 Chol (mg); 30 Carbo (g); 11 Prot (g); 45 Na (mg)
  Dietary Fiber: 7.3g
  Fat (g): 1; Sat .3; Poly .2; Mono .6
  Calories: 164
  Exchanges: 2 starch/bread; 1 lean meat

Zucchini Soup

· ·

2 cups Chicken Broth (see index)
2 cups zucchini, sliced
1 cup onion, chopped
3 cloves garlic, smashed
3 dashes dried marjoram
⅛ teaspoon cayenne pepper
Few dashes celery seed
1 teaspoon curry powder
1 tablespoon tarragon vinegar
Salt and pepper to taste
2 tablespoons non-fat dry milk
1 cup non-fat yogurt
2 tablespoons diced pimento for garnish
(optional)

Place all ingredients except last three in an 8-cup measure, and microwave on High for 8 to 10 minutes until vegetables are tender. Let cool, then puree a little at a time in a food processor or blender. Add milk and yogurt and blend. Chill before serving and garnish with pimento.

· **Serves:** 4
· **Cooking time:** 8 to 10 minutes
· **Preparation time:** 15 minutes
· **Per Serving:** 3 Chol (mg) 13 Carbo (g); 5 Prot (g);
    91 Na (mg)
   Dietary Fiber: 2.6g
   Fat (g): 0; Sat 0; Poly 0; Mono 0
   Calories: 70
   Exchanges: 1 vegetable; ½ skim milk

Fish

Out of the deep blue sea comes a source of protein that is one of the staples of a good nutrition plan. Fish is low in fat and provides essential Omega-3 oils. It is easily prepared, and the microwave proves to be an unbeatable cooking method. Fish cooked in the microwave oven, whether sauced or simply poached, retain their moisture and taste. Only a few minutes are needed to turn out a tasty and healthful dish.

Hints for Healthy Fish Preparation

- Buy only fresh-smelling fish. If it smells fishy, pass it by.

- Flesh must be firm and moist and eyes clear. Skin should look shiny but not feel slimy.

- Frozen fish retains nutrients but should not smell or contain slushy liquid or have freezer burn.

- Fish should be kept refrigerated or frozen, and it should be consumed within two days of purchase (or thawing).

- Fish is cooked when flesh has turned from translucent to opaque, and it springs back to the touch. Test fish for doneness in its thickest part by cutting into it. If it flakes when pierced with a fork, it is cooked through.

- Shrimp are cooked when they turn pink. Do not overcook.

- When arranging fish in microwave-safe baking dishes, place thicker edges toward outside and rotate dish during cooking cycle.

- Simple fish preparation might include marinating fillets with wine or lemon juice and adding spices such as basil and dill. A little dusting of paprika and pepper and some chopped fresh parsley add color to white fish.

Bluefish Florentine

1 medium onion, sliced
1 teaspoon olive oil
4 cups spinach leaves, rinsed well,
stems trimmed (or 10 ounces frozen
spinach, thawed)
1 tablespoon frozen orange juice
concentrate
1 teaspoon olive oil
1 teaspoon reduced-sodium soy sauce
1 pound bluefish fillets
Dash paprika
Dash pepper
4 thin slices lemon
Parsley, chopped, for garnish

Arrange sliced onion and olive oil on microwave-safe platter. Cover with plastic wrap and microwave on High for 2 minutes until onion is tender. Add spinach, cover, and microwave another 2 minutes on High. Let rest covered.

Meanwhile, mix together orange juice, oil, and soy sauce and drizzle over spinach. Set aside and keep warm.

Rinse fish and place in 8 x 10-inch microwave-safe baking dish. Season with paprika and pepper and cover with wax paper. Microwave on High for 3 to 4 minutes, turning once, and rotating dish.

(Please turn page)

Fish is done when it flakes easily with a fork. Remove fish and place over spinach. Top each fillet with lemon slice and parsley garnish.

· **Serves:** 4
· **Cooking time:** 7 to 8 minutes
· **Preparation time:** 15 minutes
· **Per Serving:** 50 Chol (mg);   6 Carbo (g);   19 Prot (g);
    142 Na (mg)
    Dietary Fiber: 2g
    Fat (g):   6;   Sat 1.1;   Poly 1.1;   Mono 3.0
    Calories: 154
    Exchanges: 1 vegetable;   3 lean meat

Fillet of Sole Dijonnaise

1¼ pounds fillet of sole
6 medium stalks asparagus, cut diagonally into 2-inch pieces
1 tablespoon low-fat mayonnaise
1½ tablespoons Dijon mustard
Juice of 1 lemon
1 tablespoon chopped chives (dried or frozen fresh)
Dash pepper
Few dashes paprika
Parsley, chopped, for garnish

Arrange fillets in 2-quart baking dish, tucking under thin edges, with thick parts to outside of dish. Arrange asparagus around outside of dish, with one or two stalks in-between fillets.

Mix mayonnaise, mustard, lemon, and chives and spread over fish. Sprinkle with dashes of pepper and paprika.

Microwave on High for 3 to 4 minutes, rotating and moving fillets to cook them evenly. Cover and microwave another 1 minute, until fish flakes easily with a fork. Let stand covered for another minute or two. Top fish with dusting of parsley.

· **Serves:** 4
· **Cooking time:** 4 to 5 minutes
· **Preparation time:** 15 minutes
· **Per Serving:** 87 Chol (mg);   3 Carbo (g);   28 Prot (g);   165 Na (mg)
   Dietary Fiber: 1.0 g
   Fat (g):   10;   Sat 1.5;   Poly 3.8;   Mono 3.2
   Calories: 216
   Exchanges: 4 meat

Gingered Sole

2 teaspoons low-sodium soy sauce
1 tablespoon frozen orange juice
    concentrate
1 clove garlic, minced
1 tablespoon sesame oil
2 teaspoons fresh ginger, minced
1¼ pounds fillet of sole or flounder
Dash pepper
1 teaspoon sesame seeds, toasted
Parsley, chopped, for garnish

In a small jar, mix together soy, orange juice, garlic, sesame oil, and ginger. Shake to blend and let rest at least 15 minutes to develop taste.

In an 8 x 10-inch microwave-safe dish arrange fish, tucking under any thin edges. Spoon sauce over fish and cover with wax paper. Microwave on High for 1½ to 2 minutes. Rotate dish and turn fish. Microwave on High for another 1½ to 2 minutes. Let stand a minute before uncovering, then top fish with dash of pepper, sprinkling of toasted sesame seeds, and chopped parsley.

· **Serves:** 4
· **Cooking time:** 3 to 4 minutes
· **Preparation time:** 25 minutes, including marinade resting time
· **Per Serving:** 85 Chol (mg); 2.1 Carbo (g); 27 Prot (g); 160 Na (mg)
    Dietary Fiber: .1g
    Fat (g): 12; Sat 1.8; Poly 4.6; Mono 4.5
    Calories: 232
    Exchanges: 4 lean meat

Lemon Trout

. . . .

1 pound trout fillets, cut into 4 pieces
4 slices lemon
¼ cup dry white wine
¼ cup shallots, chopped
1 teaspoon lemon peel, grated
¼ teaspoon pepper
1 tablespoon parsley, chopped
Dash cayenne

Wash fish and pat dry. Arrange with thick sides outward in an 8 x 12-inch baking dish. Top with lemon slices. Combine wine, shallots, lemon peel, pepper, and parsley and spoon mixture over fish.

Cover with wax paper, and microwave on High for 2 to 3½ minutes. Rearrange fish pieces for even cooking or rotate dish. Microwave, covered, for another 2 to 3½ minutes, until fish flakes easily with a fork. Dust with a little cayenne.

· **Serves:** 4
· **Cooking time:** 4 to 7 minutes
· **Preparation time:** 10 minutes
· **Per Serving:** 62 Chol (mg); 2 Carbo (g); 23 Prot (g);
    33 Na (mg)
    Dietary Fiber: 0.3g
    Fat (g): 4; Sat .7; Poly 1.3; Mono 1.1
    Calories: 148
    Exchanges: 3 lean meat

Lemon Halibut

· ·

1¼ pounds halibut or haddock fillets
Juice of 2 lemons
Dash of dill weed
Paprika
Pepper
Parsley sprigs for garnish

Rinse and pat dry fish, and arrange in a 2-quart oblong glass baking dish. Spoon lemon juice over fish and dust fillets with dill weed, paprika, and pepper. Cover with vented plastic wrap, and microwave on High for 2 minutes. Fish is done if it flakes easily when pierced with fork. Garnish with a few parsley sprigs.

(Any fish fillets will taste good cooked this simple way. Try it with sole, cod, snapper, or flounder.)

· Serves: 4
· Cooking time: 2 minutes
· Preparation time: 5 minutes
· Per Serving: 45 Chol (mg); 3 Carbo (g); 30 Prot (g); 83 Na (mg)
    Dietary Fiber: 0
    Fat (g): 4; Sat .5; Poly 1.2; Mono 1.0
    Calories: 163
    Exchanges: 4 lean meat

Halibut Steaks Marengo

1¼ pounds halibut steaks
Dash salt and pepper
1 medium tomato, diced
¼ cup fresh mushrooms, sliced
1¼ cup onion, sliced
¼ cup celery, diced
1 tablespoon lemon juice
1 tablespoon canola oil
¼ teaspoon dried thyme
Parsley, chopped, for garnish

Place fish in shallow baking dish and sprinkle with salt and pepper. Top with diced tomato and set aside.

In a 2-cup measure, mix mushrooms, onion, celery, lemon juice, oil, and thyme. Cover with vented plastic wrap, and microwave on High for 2 to 3 minutes. Spoon over fish.

Microwave fish, covered with wax paper, for 6 minutes on High. Halibut is cooked if it flakes easily when pierced with a fork. Garnish with fresh parsley.

· **Serves:** 4
· **Cooking time:** 9 minutes
· **Preparation time:** 10 minutes
· **Per Serving:** 46 Chol (mg);   6 Carbo (g);   31 Prot (g);
     117 Na (mg)
     Dietary Fiber: 2.1g
     Fat (g):   7;   Sat .8;   Poly 1.1;   Mono 3.4
     Calories: 214
     Exchanges: 4 lean meat;   1 vegetable

Nutty Sea Scallops

. . . .

1¼ pounds sea scallops, halved
    horizontally
½ cup dry white wine
1 small jalapeno pepper, chopped fine
1 teaspoon olive oil
2 cloves garlic, smashed, peeled, or
    minced
¼ cup shallots, chopped
Juice of ½ lemon
½ cup green peas (if frozen, thawed)
¼ cup red bell pepper, chopped
1 cup mushrooms, sliced
½ teaspoon dill weed
2 tablespoons peanuts, chopped
Parsley, chopped, for garnish

Marinate scallops in wine with jalapeno pepper for a few hours before cooking.

In an 8 x 12-inch microwave-safe dish, combine oil, garlic, and shallots, and microwave on High for 2 minutes. Add lemon juice, peas, bell pepper, mushrooms, and dill and mix well. Microwave for 2 minutes on High and stir.

Arrange scallops over cooked ingredients, and microwave on High for 2 to 3 minutes, rotating dish once. Let stand a minute before sprinkling on chopped peanuts and dusting of parsley.

· **Serves:** 4
· **Cooking time:** 6 to 7 minutes
· **Preparation time:** 20 minutes plus marinating time
· **Per Serving:** 60 Chol (mg); 7 Carbo (g); 29 Prot (g); 342 Na (mg)
  Dietary Fiber: 2.2g
  Fat (g): 4; Sat .8; Poly .8; Mono 1.6
  Calories: 200
  Exchanges: 4 lean meat; 1 vegetable

Poached Fish

1¼ pounds orange roughy fillets, or
 other white fish such as haddock,
 cod, pollock
½ cup dry white wine
Pinch salt
 ⅛ teaspoon white pepper
 ¼ teaspoon dried dill
Dash of paprika
Sprinkle of celery seed
 2 tablespoons lemon juice
 4 lemon slices for garnish
Parsley, chopped

Place fish fillets in an 8 x 8-inch glass baking dish. Pour wine over fillets and dust with spices and lemon juice. Cover with vented plastic wrap and microwave at 50% (Medium) for 10 minutes, rotating dish twice. Let stand covered for another 2 to 3 minutes. Serve warm or chilled with lemon slices, parsley garnish, or a sauce of your choice.

· **Serves:** 4
· **Cooking time:** 10 minutes
· **Preparation time:** 8 minutes
· **Per Serving:** 24 Chol (mg); 1 Carbo (g); 17 Prot (g); 102 Na (mg)
 Dietary Fiber: 0
 Fat (g): 8; Sat .2; Poly .1; Mono 3.9
 Calories: 165
 Exchanges: 3 lean meat

Salmon Tarragon

1 pound salmon fillet, cut into 4 pieces
¼ cup fresh lemon juice
½ teaspoon dried tarragon
Pepper
1 tablespoon pimentos, drained,
    chopped

Wash and pat dry fish fillets. Mix lemon juice, tarragon, and a few dashes of pepper. Arrange fish in a glass baking dish, thick sides outward, and spoon marinade over fillets. Let rest a few minutes to absorb flavor.

Cover with wax paper and microwave on Medium High (70%) for 5 to 6 minutes, until fish flakes easily when pierced with fork. Turn pieces mid-cycle for even cooking. Garnish with pimentos.

· **Serves:** 4
· **Cooking time:** 5 to 6 minutes
· **Preparation time:** 10 minutes
· **Per Serving:** 75 Chol (mg); 2 Carbo (g); 24 Prot (g);
    60 Na (mg)
    Dietary Fiber: 0
    Fat (g): 9; Sat 1.7; Poly 2.1; Mono 4.5
    Calories: 188
    Exchanges: 3 lean meat

Teriyaki Sea Scallops

2 tablespoons dry sherry
1 tablespoon low-sodium soy sauce
2 tablespoons water
1 tablespoon sesame oil
2 teaspoons ginger root, fresh grated
1 teaspoon frozen orange juice concentrate
2 cloves garlic, minced
1 pound sea scallops
1 tablespoon lemon juice
Paprika
Parsley, chopped, for garnish

Combine sherry, soy sauce, water, oil, ginger, orange juice, and garlic in 8 x 10-inch glass baking dish. Add scallops and marinate in refrigerator up to four hours, turning to coat, or at room temperature for one-half hour.

When ready to cook, cover with vented plastic wrap, and microwave on High for 2 to 3 minutes. Turn scallops over and rotate dish; then microwave on High another 2 to 3 minutes. Scallops are cooked when they turn opaque. Let sit, covered, for 3 minutes. Spoon lemon juice over scallops, dust with paprika, and sprinkle on fresh parsley.

- **Serves:** 4
- **Cooking time:** 4 to 6 minutes
- **Preparation time:** 10 minutes plus marinating time
- **Per Serving:** 45 Chol (mg); 2 Carbo (g); 20 Prot (g);
      380 Na (mg)
      Dietary Fiber: 0
      Fat (g): 5; Sat 1; Poly 1.7; Mono 1.8
      Calories: 137
      Exchanges: 3 lean meat

Meat

Beef has been banned from many dietary regimens because of its contribution to high cholesterol. But every so often I yearn to sink my teeth into something other than fish, chicken, or tofu. So a few of my favorite meat recipes are included here for others who are infrequently tempted to "bite the beef." In each case, low fat cuts of meat, well trimmed, have been chosen, and the portions are reasonable. Eaten in moderation, a meat treat will provide additional nutrients.

Attila's Beef Goulash

1 pound boneless, lean beef chuck,
trimmed of all fat, cut into 1-inch
cubes
3 medium onions, chopped
1 large green bell pepper, chopped
(about 2 cups)
3 cloves garlic, minced
1 teaspoon olive oil
2 tablespoons Hungarian paprika
¼ teaspoon salt
¼ teaspoon black pepper
1 tablespoon balsamic vinegar
1 cup tomato sauce
1 cup fresh mushrooms, sliced

Heat browning dish for 5 minutes on High. When
ready, remove from oven and place beef cubes on
dish, turning as they brown. Microwave on High for
4 minutes, stirring once. Drain.

Place onions, green pepper, garlic, and oil in a
2-quart measure and microwave on High 5 minutes,
stirring once or twice. Meantime, combine paprika,
salt, and pepper and stir into meat. Add vinegar
and tomato sauce.

When vegetables are soft, turn meat mixture
into measuring cup and stir to blend. Cover with
vented plastic wrap, and microwave on High for 5
minutes. Stir and return to oven. Microwave on
Medium (50%) for 30 minutes, stirring a few times.
During last 10 minutes, add mushrooms.

Let rest 5 to 10 minutes before serving with noodles, rice, or potatoes. (Goulash is even better if served the following day.)

For a variation, add ¼ cup non-fat plain yogurt if desired.

· **Serves:** 4
· **Cooking time:** 44 minutes plus preheating time
· **Preparation time:** 25 minutes
· **Per Serving:** 90 Chol (mg); 15 Carbo (g); 29 Prot (g);
      545 Na (mg)
      Dietary Fiber: 4.8 g
      Fat (g): 15; Sat 5.5; Poly .8; Mono 6.6
      Calories: 309
      Exchanges: 3 medium-fat meat; 2 vegetable

Creole Pork Chops

4 loin pork chops, 1-inch thick (about 1 pound)
1 medium onion, chopped
1 small green bell pepper, cut into strips
½ cup celery, sliced thin on diagonal
2 tablespoons parsley, chopped
1 teaspoon chopped green chili peppers (canned)
Dash salt and pepper
2 cloves garlic, minced
1 14-ounce can stewed tomatoes, drained

Trim all fat off chops, rinse, and pat dry. Arrange in 12-inch-square glass baking dish, thick parts to the outside. Add onions, pepper, celery, parsley, and chili peppers. Cover with vented plastic wrap, and microwave at Medium-high (70%) for 5 minutes. Rotate dish, turn chops over, and microwave at 70% for another 5 minutes.

Add remaining ingredients, cover with vented plastic wrap, and microwave on Medium-high (70%) for another 15 minutes, until chops are cooked through. Let stand covered for 5 to 10 minutes before serving.

· **Serves:** 4
· **Cooking time:** 25 minutes
· **Preparation time:** 25 minutes
· **Per Serving:** 77 Chol (mg);   12 Carbo (g);   25 Prot (g);   386 Na (mg)
   Dietary Fiber: 2.5 g
   Fat (g):   12;   Sat 4.2;   Poly 1.6;   Mono 5.4
   Calories: 254
   Exchanges: 3 medium-fat meat;   2 vegetable

Gingered Indian Lamb

1 pound lean lamb
¼ cup ginger root, chopped fine
1 medium onion, chopped rough
4 cloves garlic, peeled and smashed
8 ounces canned Italian plum tomatoes,
  drained
Juice of ½ lemon
¼ teaspoon turmeric
¼ teaspoon celery seed
½ teaspoon cumin
1 tablespoon curry powder, mild or hot
¼ cup non-fat plain yogurt
1 cup frozen peas
½ cup fresh mushrooms, sliced
  (optional)

Trim all fat from lamb and cut, against the grain,
into 1-inch pieces. Place ginger root, onions, garlic,
and tomatoes in 8 x 10-inch glass baking dish, and
cover with vented plastic wrap. Microwave on High
for 2 minutes. Remove wrap and stir in all remaining ingredients except peas and mushrooms.

(Please turn page)

Cover and refrigerate a few hours or overnight. Stir from time to time. When ready to prepare for meal, remove from refrigerator and let rest at room temperature about half an hour. Then cover with vented plastic wrap and microwave on High for 5 minutes. Add peas and mushrooms, and microwave another 1 minute until warmed through.

- **Serves:** 4
- **Cooking time:** 8 minutes
- **Preparation time:** 15 minutes plus refrigerating and resting time
- **Per Serving:** 81 Chol (mg); 13 Carbo (g); 29 Prot (g); 219 Na (mg)
  Dietary Fiber: 4.0 g
  Fat (g): 4; Sat 3.4; Poly .7; Mono 4.2
  Calories: 256
  Exchanges: 4 lean meat; 1 starch/bread

Meat Loaf Marvel

1 pound 90% lean ground beef (preferably round)
¼ cup green pepper, chopped
¼ cup red pepper, chopped
¾ cup onion, chopped
3 cloves garlic, minced
½ cup whole wheat bread crumbs
1 tablespoon reduced-sodium soy sauce
1 tablespoon Dijon mustard
Dash black pepper
1 Vlasic baby dill pickle, chopped

Mix all ingredients together and mold into a long,
round loaf, about 2-inches deep. Arrange in circle
on a 9-inch pie plate or deep casserole. Microwave
on High for 3 to 4 minutes. Baste with sauce and
drain off excess. After rotating plate, microwave on
High another 3 to 4 minutes.

· **Serves:** 4
· **Cooking time:** 6 to 8 minutes
· **Preparation time:** 20 minutes
· **Per Serving:** 84 Chol (mg);   15 Carbo (g);   23 Prot (g);
      394 Na (mg)
      Dietary Fiber: 1.6 g
      Fat (g):   21;   Sat 9.6;   Poly 1.2;   Mono 9.8
      Calories: 335
      Exchanges: 3 medium-fat meat;   1 starch/bread;
         1 fat

Oriental Sliced Beef

2 tablespoons reduced-sodium soy sauce
2 tablespoons water
1 teaspoon sesame oil
1 clove garlic, minced
1 teaspoon Dijon mustard
1 teaspoon fresh ginger root, grated
1 pound lean flank steak, sliced thin
   across the grain (this is done more
   easily if steak is partially frozen)
1 red bell pepper, julienned
4 scallions, chopped
1 teaspoon toasted sesame seeds
Parsley, chopped, for garnish

Blend first six ingredients and place in a 2-quart casserole. Add sliced meat and stir to coat. Mix in peppers and scallions. Microwave on High 3 to 4 minutes, stirring once. Remove from oven and check for doneness. Some pieces may be more rare than others, and your choice will dictate further cooking for another minute or so. Garnish with sesame seeds and chopped parsley.

- Serves: 4
- Cooking time: 3 to 5 minutes
- Preparation time: 15 minutes
- Per Serving: 60 Chol (mg);   3 Carbo (g);   23 Prot (g);
   389 Na (mg)
   Dietary Fiber: 1.0g
   Fat (g):   15;   Sat 5.7;   Poly 1.1;   Mono 6.0
   Calories: 236
   Exchanges: 3 medium-fat meat

Poultry

The great advantage of chicken and turkey is
their low cholesterol levels. They also are easy to
microwave, but care must be taken that all the
pieces are cooked through so that there is no risk
of salmonella. For the same reason poultry should
never be allowed to sit at room temperature for
any length of time. Be sure to wash any utensils
and surfaces that come in contact with uncooked
poultry. Use a polyurethane cutting board rather
than a wooden one, and rinse meat in cold water
before cooking.

My preference is for boneless and skinless
poultry cutlets. However, it may be more economi-
cal to buy breasts with the bone in, in which case
you will need to remove the skin and cut away
the bone. If using a whole chicken, remove the
skin by pointing the bird's legs toward you, grasp-
ing the skin (using paper toweling), and pulling

the skin back from the neck. Cut the skin if necessary and discard.

Poultry combines well with vegetables and a variety of sauces; it may be served alone or with rice, pasta, or potatoes. Poaching boneless chicken or turkey cutlets provides readily cooked morsels for use in a variety of recipes.

To insure even cooking, slice or cut the poultry into small, evenly sized pieces, and be sure to turn them during the microwaving process. However chicken or turkey is prepared, it is a nutritious, low-fat, versatile protein.

Chicken Paprikash

1 pound skinless, boneless
  chicken breast
1 teaspoon canola oil
2 medium onions, chopped fine
2 cloves garlic, minced
1 medium green pepper, chopped
1 cup mushrooms, sliced
1 cup stewed tomatoes, crushed
2½ to 3 teaspoons sweet Hungarian
  paprika
1 teaspoon poppy seeds
¼ cup Yogurt Sour Cream (see
  index)
Salt and pepper to taste

Cut the chicken (against the grain) into thin slices. Heat a browning dish on High for 5 minutes, or follow manufacturer's directions. brown chicken slices a few at a time and set aside.

Place oil, onions, garlic, and green pepper in a 1-quart measure or casserole and microwave on High for 3 minutes, stirring. Add mushrooms and microwave on High another 2 minutes. Mix in tomatoes and paprika, stir to combine, and then add chicken and poppy seeds.

(Please turn page)

Cover with wax paper and microwave on High for 4 to 5 minutes, stirring once. Remove, let rest a few minutes, then add yogurt sour cream and adjust seasoning. Serve over noodles or rice.

- **Serves:** 4
- **Cooking time:** 9 to 10 minutes plus preheating time
- **Preparation time:** 15 minutes
- **Per Serving:** 73 Chol (mg);   13 Carbo (g);   30 Prot (g);   277 Na (mg)
    Dietary Fiber: 3.3g
    Fat (g):   5;   Sat 1.1;   Poly .9;   Mono 1.9
    Calories: 211
    Exchanges: 4 lean meat;   2 vegetable

Chicken Salad

12 ounces Poached Chicken Breasts (see index)
4 scallions, sliced
3 teaspoons dried basil
1 cup low-fat plain yogurt
2 teaspoons tomato paste
1 teaspoon capers and 1 teaspoon caper juice
Pepper
1 bunch watercress
4 large romaine leaves

Cut chicken diagonally into thin slices or into small chunks. Place in bowl and add scallions and basil. Mix the yogurt, tomato paste, capers, and caper juice and season with pepper.

Trim watercress of tough stems. Chop one-quarter of the bunch and mix it in with the chicken. Combine chicken and yogurt sauce, and serve over romaine leaves. Garnish with remaining watercress.

· **Serves:** 4
· **Cooking time:** 8 to 10 minutes poaching time
· **Preparation time:** 15 minutes
· **Per Serving:** 73 Chol (mg);   5 Carbo (g);   30 Prot (g);   150 Na (mg)
   Dietary Fiber: 2.3g
   Fat (g):   3;   Sat 1.0;   Poly .7;   Mono 1.1
   Calories: 175
   Exchanges: 4 lean meat;   1 vegetable

Chicken Tarragon

1 pound skinless, boneless chicken
   breast
2 tablespoons low-sodium soy sauce
   mixed with 2 tablespoons water
Juice of 1 lemon
2 cloves garlic, minced
1 teaspoon sesame oil
2 teaspoons dried tarragon
Pepper

Trim chicken of any fat and cut into cubes or thin slices. Combine with soy sauce and lemon juice and let marinate 15 minutes.

Place garlic and sesame oil in a 1-cup measure and microwave for 1 minute on High. In a 1-quart casserole, combine oil and garlic with chicken marinade, add tarragon and pepper, and cover with vented plastic wrap. Microwave on Medium (50%) for 4 to 6 minutes, stirring, until chicken is cooked through.

· Serves: 4
· Cooking time: 5 to 7 minutes
· Preparation time: 10 minutes plus marinating time
· Per Serving: 72 Chol (mg);   3 Carbo (g);   27 Prot (g);
      368 Na (mg)
   Dietary Fiber: 0
   Fat (g):   4;   Sat 1.0;   Poly 1.2;   Mono 1.5
   Calories: 164
   Exchanges: 4 lean meat

Chili con Chicken

12 ounces skinless, boneless chicken
  breasts
3 tablespoons lemon juice
1 teaspoon virgin olive oil
2 cloves garlic, minced
2 medium onions, sliced
2 bell peppers (red and green),
  julienned
1 teaspoon ground cumin
1½ teaspoons dried oregano
2 teaspoons fresh chili pepper, finely
  chopped, or 1 teaspoon dried hot
  pepper flakes
½ teaspoon pepper
2 tablespoons parsley, chopped, for
  garnish

Slice chicken into half-inch strips and sprinkle with
lemon juice. Set aside. Place the oil, garlic, and onion in 2-quart casserole, and microwave on High,
uncovered, for 2 minutes. Add pepper strips, cumin, oregano, and chili. Mix, cover with wax paper,
and microwave on High for another 2 minutes, stirring once. Transfer to a serving platter.

(Please turn page)

Top vegetables with chicken strips. Cover with wax paper and microwave on High for 2 to 3 minutes; then turn chicken pieces. Microwave on High for another 1 to 2 minutes, until chicken is no longer pink. Season with pepper and garnish with parsley.

· **Serves:** 4
· **Cooking time:** 7 to 9 minutes
· **Preparation time:** 20 minutes
· **Per Serving:** 60 Chol (mg);   6 Carbo (g);   23 Prot (g);   168 Na (mg)
    Dietary Fiber: 0
    Fat (g): 6;   Sat 1.2;   Poly 1.0;   Mono 3.4
    Calories: 174
    Exchanges: 3 lean meat;   1 vegetable

Cantonese Chicken

12 ounces skinless, boneless chicken
   breasts
1 cup broccoli florets
1 cup cauliflower florets
½ pound mushrooms, sliced
4 scallions, cut into 1-inch pieces
2 tablespoons low-sodium soy sauce
3 tablespoons dry sherry
1 teaspoon ginger, fresh grated
1 teaspoon arrowroot dissolved in 2
   tablespoons water
1 teaspoon sesame oil
¼ cup unsalted peanuts

Trim all fat off chicken and slice thinly on diagonal.
Arrange slices on a flat baking dish, cover with
microwave-safe wax paper, and microwave on High
for 6 to 8 minutes, turning, until cooked through.
Set aside and keep warm, wrapped in foil.

(Please turn page)

Combine broccoli, cauliflower, mushrooms, scallions, soy sauce, sherry, and ginger in a 2-quart measure. Microwave on High for 6 to 10 minutes, stirring. Add dissolved arrowroot, sesame oil, peanuts, and the chicken pieces. Stir to combine, and microwave on High for 2 minutes until warmed through.

· **Serves:** 4
· **Cooking time:** 14 to 20 minutes
· **Preparation time:** 20 minutes
· **Per Serving:** 72 Chol (mg);   9 Carbo (g);   26 Prot (g);
     365 Na (mg)
     Dietary Fiber: 3.5g
     Fat (g):   9;   Sat 1.6;   Poly 1.8;   Mono 4.4
     Calories: 223
     Exchanges: 3 lean meat;   2 vegetable

Chicken Crunch

1 frying chicken, 2½ to 3 pounds
1 cup buttermilk
½ teaspoon garlic powder
½ teaspoon paprika (hot or mild)
¼ teaspoon thyme
¼ teaspoon salt
2 cups NutriGrain Cornflakes, finely crushed

Cut chicken into pieces and remove skin with help of paper toweling. Rinse and pat dry. Dip chicken pieces into buttermilk.

Combine all spices and crushed cornflakes in a paper bag. Shake chicken pieces in the bag until coated, and place in 12-inch glass baking dish with thicker pieces toward outside.

Cover with wax paper. Microwave on High for 7 to 8 minutes, then turn chicken pieces and rotate dish. Microwave on High another 6 to 8 minutes.

· **Serves:** 6
· **Cooking time:** 13 to 16 minutes
· **Preparation time:** 14 to 16 minutes
· **Per Serving:** 102 Chol (mg); 8 Carbo (g); 35 Prot (g); 304 Na (mg)
  Dietary Fiber: 0
  Fat (g): 9; Sat 2.5; Poly 1.9; Mono 3.1
  Calories: 260
  Exchanges: 4 lean meat; ½ starch/bread

Chicken Paillards

1 pound boneless, skinless chicken
   breasts, halved
Salt to taste
½ teaspoon black pepper
1 teaspoon whipped butter
1 teaspoon canola oil
¼ cup Chicken Broth (see index)
2 cloves garlic, minced
2 tablespoons fresh lemon juice
4 slices lemon
Paprika
2 tablespoons parsley, chopped, for
   garnish

Place chicken between two sheets of wax paper and
pound to half-inch thick *paillards*. Season each side
of chicken with salt and pepper, and set aside in
baking dish.

Place butter and oil in a 1-cup glass measure,
and microwave on 50% for 1 minute, until butter
melts. Combine with chicken stock, garlic, and
lemon juice. Spoon juice over chicken, cover with
wax paper, and microwave on High for 5 to 6
minutes, turning once and rotating dish.

Chicken is done when it is no longer pink. Top each *paillard* with a lemon slice, a dash of paprika and parsley garnish, and spoon sauce over each piece.

· **Serves:** 4
· **Cooking time:** 6 to 7 minutes
· **Preparation time:** 15 minutes
· **Per Serving:** 76 Chol (mg);   1 Carbo (g);   26 Prot (g);
     135 Na (mg)
     Dietary Fiber: 0
     Fat (g):   7;   Sat 2.1;   Poly 2.2;   Mono 2.1
     Calories: 189
     Exchanges: 4 lean meat

Poached Chicken Breasts

1 pound boneless, skinless chicken
  breasts
1 lemon, sliced thinly
Few sprigs parsley

Trim fat from cutlets. Pound to even thickness of
about one-half inch between two pieces of wax paper. Arrange in 2-quart glass baking dish, with
thicker sides to outside. Add lemon and parsley.

Cover with vented plastic wrap, and microwave
on High for 4 to 5 minutes. Flip cutlets over and
microwave on High for another 4 to 5 minutes.
Poultry is cooked when juices run clear when
pricked with a fork. (One pound of boneless chicken
breast yields 2 cups of cut-up cooked chicken.)

Turkey cutlets may be prepared in the same
way, although the time will be a little shorter.
Poaching a pound of turkey cutlets should take 5 to
8 minutes on High.

· **Serves:** 4
· **Cooking time:** 8 to 10 minutes
· **Preparation time:** 5 minutes
· **Per Serving:** 72 Chol (mg); 1 Carbo (g); 27 Prot (g);
     67 Na (mg)
    Dietary Fiber: 0
    Fat (g): 3; Sat .9; Poly .7; Mono 1.0
    Calories: 145
    Exchanges: 4 lean meat

Sesame Chicken

¼ cup reduced-sodium soy sauce
1 scallion, sliced
1 tablespoon Dijon mustard
1 teaspoon sesame oil
1 tablespoon fresh ginger root, chopped
1 tablespoon frozen orange juice
    concentrate
1 pound boneless, skinless chicken
    breast, cut into 1-inch cubes
1 tablespoon toasted sesame seeds
1 tablespoon parsley, chopped

Mix together first six ingredients in 1-quart measure. Add chicken and marinate for at least 1 hour, turning a few times. When ready to cook, remove chicken and arrange it in a 9-inch baking dish.

Cover with wax paper and microwave on High for 3 to 4 minutes. Turn chicken pieces, cover again, and microwave on High for another 3 to 4 minutes. Chicken is done when it is white. Sprinkle with sesame seeds and parsley.

· **Serves:** 4
· **Cooking time:** 6 to 8 minutes
· **Preparation time:** 15 minutes plus marinating time
· **Per Serving:** 72 Chol (mg);   4 Carbo (g);   28 Prot (g);
      711 Na (mg)
    Dietary Fiber: 0
    Fat (g):   5;   Sat 1.2;   Poly 1.6;   Mono 1.9
    Calories: 180
    Exchanges: 4 lean meat

South Indian Chicken Curry

2 stalks celery, chopped (about 1 cup)
½ cup green pepper, chopped
¾ cup fresh mushrooms, chopped
3 cloves garlic, minced
1 small onion, chopped
1 tablespoon fresh ginger root, minced
1 tablespoon olive oil
⅛ teaspoon turmeric
¼ teaspoon ground cumin
1 tablespoon mild curry powder
½ cup non-fat plain yogurt
1 pound skinless, boneless chicken breast, sliced thinly on diagonal

Place first 6 ingredients and oil in 1-quart glass measure and microwave on High for 3 minutes, stirring once. Mix spices with yogurt. Turn all ingredients, including chicken into a casserole and let marinate for several hours.

Before cooking, bring to room temperature. Cover with lid or paper towels, and microwave on High for 3 to 4 minutes. Stir and return to microwave; cook on High another 3 to 4 minutes. Serve with basmati rice, noodles, or on top of baked potato halves.

· **Serves:** 4
· **Cooking time:** 9 to 11 minutes
· **Preparation time:** 20 minutes plus marinating time
· **Per Serving:** 73 Chol (mg);   6 Carbo (g);   29 Prot (g);
    113 Na (mg)
    Dietary Fiber: 1.9g
    Fat (g):   7;   Sat 1.4;   Poly 1.0;   Mono 3.6
    Calories: 203
    Exchanges: 4 lean meat;   1 vegetable

Turkey Peppercorn

1 pound turkey breast cutlets, pounded
to ¼-inch thickness
1 tablespoon black (or green) peppercorns, crushed in blender
½ cup dry white wine
1 tablespoon brandy
1 tablespoon parsley, chopped, for
garnish

Rinse turkey cutlets and pat dry. Press crushed
peppercorns firmly into both sides of turkey cutlets.
Smack cutlets with the side of a cleaver or saute
pan to make peppercorns adhere. Place cutlets in
12-inch glass casserole, and add wine and brandy.
Microwave on High for 2 to 3 minutes. Stir. Serve
with garnish of parsley.

· Serves: 4
· Cooking time: 2 to 3 minutes
· Preparation time: 10 minutes
· Per Serving: 78 Chol (mg);   1 Carbo (g);   25 Prot (g);
     68 Na (mg)
   Dietary Fiber: 0
   Fat (g): 1; Sat .2; Poly .2; Mono .1
   Calories: 158
   Exchanges: 4 lean meat

Turkey Marsala

12 ounces turkey breast cutlets, sliced
   thin on diagonal
1 teaspoon dried rosemary, crushed
2 tablespoons Marsala (or sherry)
¼ cup dry white wine
Pepper
Parsley sprigs for garnish

Heat a browning dish on High for 5 minutes in the microwave. Place half of turkey slices on dish, and microwave on High for 1 to 2 minutes. Repeat with remaining turkey slices. Combine turkey slices and microwave on High until no longer pink, about 1 minute.

Mix rosemary and wine and let steep a few minutes. When turkey is white, add wine mixture and microwave another 1 to 2 minutes on High. Season with fresh pepper and serve with parsley garnish. Let stand a few minutes before serving.

· **Serves:** 4
· **Cooking time:** 4 to 7 minutes plus preheating time
· **Preparation time:** 10 minutes
· **Per Serving:** 75 Chol (mg);   1 Carbo (g);   26 Prot (g);
      57 Na (mg)
   Dietary Fiber: 0
   Fat (g):   1;   Sat .2;   Poly .2;   Mono .1
   Calories: 135
   Exchanges: 3 lean meat

Turkey Teriyaki

1 pound turkey breast or skinless,
  boneless chicken breasts
2 tablespoons low-sodium soy sauce
  mixed with 2 tablespoons water
1 tablespoon Dijon mustard
2 tablespoons fresh ginger root, grated
2 cloves garlic, minced
1 tablespoon orange rind, grated
1 teaspoon sesame oil
¼ cup dry sherry
2 cups mushrooms, sliced
1 cup green peas (if frozen, thawed)

Wash the turkey or chicken and pat dry. Cut into half-inch cubes. Blend remaining ingredients, except mushrooms and peas, and pour over turkey. Let turkey marinate for at least 1 hour or, preferably, overnight in refrigerator. Turn several times.

Place mushrooms in 1-quart measure, and microwave on High for 2 minutes until soft. Drain and reserve.

Place turkey with some of marinade in 8-inch-square baking dish and cover with wax paper. Microwave on High 2 to 3 minutes. Turn poultry pieces and rotate dish. Microwave on High another 2 to 3 minutes.

Add mushrooms and peas, and microwave on High for another 1 to 2 minutes until warmed through. Serve with rice or noodles.

- **Serves:** 4
- **Cooking time:** 7 to 10 minutes
- **Preparation time:** 10 minutes plus marinating time
- **Per Serving:** 72 Chol (mg);   9 Carbo (g);   29 Prot (g);   430 Na (mg)
    Dietary Fiber: 3.2g
    Fat (g):   2;   Sat .4;   Poly .8;   Mono .6
    Calories: 183
    Exchanges: 4 lean meat;   ½ starch/bread

Grains

Grains provide many minerals and vitamins and may be prepared in myriad ways. Many of them can be main dishes, with the addition of vegetables, bits of fish or poultry, nuts, or low-fat cheese. Grains are also adaptable as desserts, in addition to their usual use as side dishes.

The microwave makes cooking grains a matter of minutes rather than long, stove-top simmering. A creamy risotto made with arborio rice is now a simple matter, and wild rice (which is actually a grass) and barley become delectable in short order. Try quinoa, an ancient Peruvian grain that has many health-giving qualities. You'll enjoy these complex-carbohydrate recipes as a welcome change from potatoes and pasta.

Bulgur Pilaf à l'Orange

¼ cup currants
2 tablespoons sunflower seeds or slivered almonds
Rind and juice of 1 orange
¾ cup bulgur or cracked wheat (3 cups cooked)
1 teaspoon sesame oil
1 small onion, chopped
1½ cups water

In a blender, process currants, sunflower seeds, orange rind, and juice. Set aside. Place bulgur, sesame oil, and onion in an 8-cup measure, and microwave on High for 2 minutes. Stir.

In another cup, bring water to boil on High (5 to 6 minutes); then add water to bulgur and microwave on High for 5 minutes. Combine with orange mixture, reduce power to Medium (50%), and microwave for 12 to 14 minutes. Let stand until liquid is absorbed. Makes 4 cups.

· Serves: 6
· Cooking time: 24 to 27 minutes
· Preparation time: 15 minutes plus standing time
· Per Serving: 0 Chol (mg);   22 Carbo (g);   4 Prot (g);
   1 Na (mg)
   Dietary Fiber: 1.6g
   Fat (g):   4;   Sat .4;   Poly 2.1;   Mono .8
   Calories: 131
   Exchanges: 1½ starch/bread; 1½ fat

Fluffy Kasha

1¾ cups water
2 teaspoons sesame oil
½ cup kasha (buckwheat groats)
1 egg white
2 cloves garlic, smashed
1 teaspoon reduced-sodium soy sauce
2 teaspoons sesame seeds
Pepper to taste

Bring water to boil, microwaving on High for 5 to 6 minutes. In another 2-quart measure, mix the sesame oil and kasha. Microwave for 1 to 2 minutes until toasted. Stir in egg white and microwave on High another 30 seconds.

Add boiling water and simmer on High 2 minutes. Add garlic and soy sauce and microwave on High for another 30 seconds. Let stand for 5 minutes. Add sesame seeds, season with pepper, and fluff with a fork.

Variation: microwave one-half cup each mushrooms, onions, and celery with a teaspoon of sesame oil for 2 minutes until tender, and fluff in when kasha is cooked. Peas, zucchini, and spinach may also be combined with groats.

· **Serves:** 4
· **Cooking time:** 9 to 11 minutes
· **Preparation time:** 5 minutes plus standing time
· **Per Serving:** 0 Chol (mg);   17 Carbo (g);   4 Prot (g);
      86 Na (mg)
      Dietary Fiber: .6g
      Fat (g):   3;   Sat .4;   Poly 1.2;   Mono 1.2
      Calories: 109
      Exchanges: 1 starch/bread

Golden Barley

2 cups water
½ cup pearl barley
1 tablespoon golden raisins
1 tablespoon almonds
1 tablespoon peanuts
¼ cup celery, chopped
Pinch ground cardamom
Salt and pepper to taste

Bring water to boil in 1-quart microwave measure and add barley. Cook on High for 30 minutes, stirring a few times. When barley is tender, drain and stir in remaining ingredients. Serve warm or chilled as a salad. Dressing may be added as desired.

· Serves: 4
· Cooking time: 30 minutes
· Preparation time: 5 minutes
· Per Serving: 0 Chol (mg); 22 Carbo (g); 2 Prot (g);
    34 Na (mg)
    Dietary Fiber: 3.2g
    Fat (g): 1; Sat .1; Poly .2; Mono .4
    Calories: 103
    Exchanges: 1½ starch/bread; 1 vegetable

Green Pea Risotto

. . . .

1¾ cups Chicken Broth (see index)
1 tablespoon olive oil
1 tablespoon whipped butter
1 onion, chopped fine
¾ cup arborio rice
2 tablespoons dry white wine
½ cup frozen peas, thawed
2 tablespoons Parmesan or Romano
    cheese, grated
Salt and pepper to taste

Place broth in a 4-cup measure, and microwave on High for 3 to 4 minutes, until it simmers. Place oil, butter, and onion in 1-quart measure, and microwave on High for 2 minutes, until onions are soft. Add rice and stir to coat.

Pour in hot chicken broth and wine. Cover with vented plastic wrap. Microwave on High for 4 to 5 minutes, until boiling. Microwave on Medium (50%) for 7 to 9 minutes more until rice is tender. Rotate dish, stir in peas, and let stand covered 5 minutes. Stir in cheese and season with salt and pepper.

· **Serves:** 6
· **Cooking time:** 16 to 20 minutes
· **Preparation time:** 7 minutes plus standing time
· **Per Serving:** 4 Chol (mg);   22 Carbo (g);   3 Prot (g);
    235 Na (mg)
    Dietary Fiber: 1.6g
    Fat (g):   4;   Sat 1.3;   Poly .3;   Mono 2.1
    Calories: 146
    Exchanges: 1½ starch/bread;   1 fat

Jane's Millet Primavera

¾ cup millet (available in natural food
   stores)
2 tablespoons olive oil
1 medium onion, chopped
2 stalks celery, diced
1 green or red pepper, diced
1 carrot, diced
1 small zucchini, diced (about ½ cup)
2 cloves garlic, minced
1 teaspoon fresh ginger root, diced
2½ cups Chicken Broth (see index)
1 teaspoon curry powder (or more if
   desired)
½ teaspoon dried dill weed
Salt and pepper to taste

Spread millet on a 9-inch pie plate, and toast in
microwave on High for 1 minute. In a 2-quart casserole or measure combine next eight ingredients,
and microwave on High for 3 to 4 minutes.

Add toasted millet and chicken broth, along with curry and dill weed. Cover with vented plastic wrap, and microwave on High for 20 minutes, stirring a few times. When grain is tender, season with salt and pepper to taste. Makes 3½ cups.

· **Serves:** 6
· **Cooking time:** 24 to 25 minutes
· **Preparation time:** 20 minutes
· **Per Serving:** 0 Chol (mg);   22 Carbo (g);   3 Prot (g);   284 Na (mg)
   Dietary Fiber: 2.3g
   Fat (g):   5;   Sat .8;   Poly .8;   Mono 3.9
   Calories: 130
   Exchanges: 1 vegetable;   1 starch/bread;   1 fat

Matzo Meal Polenta

2 cups Chicken Broth (see index)
Generous pinch turmeric
⅔ cup matzo meal
½ teaspoon hot red pepper flakes
Salt and pepper to taste
1 cup mushrooms, sliced
½ cup onions, sliced
1 teaspoon olive oil
1 teaspoon Romano cheese, grated
Tomato sauce (optional)

In a 2-quart measure, microwave broth on High for 3 minutes, until it boils. Add turmeric and stir. Add matzo meal, red pepper flakes, salt, and pepper, and microwave on High for 2 to 4 minutes, stirring once, until all liquid is absorbed. Turn into serving dish.

Place mushrooms and onions in a 2-cup bowl with olive oil, and microwave on High for 1 to 2 minutes, until tender. Top the matzo meal polenta with the vegetables and a dusting of cheese. Tomato sauce may also be used as topping if desired. May be served chilled.

- **Serves:** 6
- **Cooking time:** 6 to 9 minutes
- **Preparation time:** 10 minutes
- **Per Serving:** 0 Chol (mg);   10 Carbo (g);   2 Prot (g);   95 Na (mg)
    Dietary Fiber: 1.0g
    Fat (g):   1;   Sat .2;   Poly .5   Mono .3
    Calories: 54
    Exchanges: 1 starch/bread

Pimento Polenta

2 cups Chicken Broth (see index)
½ cup yellow cornmeal
½ cup corn niblets, drained (fresh,
    canned, or frozen)
1 tablespoon olive oil
Pinch salt
¼ teaspoon cayenne
½ teaspoon dried thyme
½ teaspoon dried oregano
2 tablespoons Parmesan cheese, grated
Dash pepper
¼ cup pimentos, sliced, for garnish

Place chicken broth in a 2-quart microwave-safe bowl, and microwave on High for 4 to 6 minutes to heat. To the broth, add cornmeal, niblets, olive oil, and next four seasonings. Microwave uncovered on High for 12 to 15 minutes, stirring every 5 minutes. When polenta is tender and liquid is absorbed, stir in Parmesan cheese and pepper. Spoon into serving dish and top with pimentos.

(Please turn page)

Variations:

1. Slice and serve with topping of salsa or tomato sauce.
2. Add microwaved onions, red or green peppers, and sliced mushrooms.
3. Mix with a little blue cheese, Gorgonzola, or goat cheese.
4. Top with part-skim ricotta and a few cooked green peas or chopped broccoli.

· **Serves:** 4
· **Cooking time:** 16 to 20 minutes
· **Preparation time:** 10 minutes
· **Per Serving:** 3 Chol (mg); 21 Carbo (g); 4 Prot (g); 123 Na (mg)
   Dietary Fiber: 3.2g
   Fat (g): 5; Sat 1.0; Poly .5; Mono 2.9
   Calories: 134
   Exchanges: 1½ starch/bread; 1 fat

Inca Pilaf

¼ cup red bell pepper, diced
2 cloves garlic, minced
1 small onion, chopped
1 teaspoon sesame oil
¾ cup quinoa (once eaten by the Incas, it is now available in natural food stores and some supermarkets; pronounced "keen-wa")
1½ cups Chicken Broth (see index)
½ cup green peas

Place pepper, garlic, onion, and sesame oil in a 4-cup glass measure. Microwave uncovered on High for 2 minutes, and stir. Add quinoa and broth and microwave on High for 5 minutes, stirring once. Microwave on Medium (50%) for 15 minutes. Add peas; stir to mix. Microwave on High another 2 minutes or until liquid is absorbed. Grains should be pearly, with white outline visible. Fluff with a fork.

· Serves: 4
· **Cooking time:** 24 minutes
· **Preparation time:** 10 minutes
· **Per Serving:** 0 Chol (mg); 17 Carbo (g); 3 Prot (g);
     289 Na (mg)
     Dietary Fiber: 2.1g
     Fat (g): 2; Sat .2; Poly .6 Mono .5
     Calories: 93
     Exchanges: 1 starch/bread

Piquant Couscous

1 cup orange juice
½ cup water
1 cup Moroccan couscous
½ teaspoon orange zest, grated
⅛ teaspoon ground cardamom
Few dashes ground ginger
1 teaspoon poppy seeds
2 tablespoons non-fat plain yogurt
1 tablespoon pecans, chopped
1 teaspoon coconut, shredded

Combine all ingredients, except last three, in a 1-quart casserole. Microwave on High for 5 minutes or until all liquid is absorbed, stirring mid-cycle. Let rest 5 minutes before stirring in yogurt. Garnish with pecans and coconut.

· **Serves:** 4
· **Cooking time:** 5 minutes
· **Preparation time:** 5 minutes plus resting time
· **Per Serving:** 0 Chol (mg); 28 Carbo (g); 5 Prot (g);
     17 Na (mg)
     Dietary Fiber: .8g
     Fat (g): 1; Sat .2; Poly .1; Mono .4
     Calories: 142
     Exchanges: 2 starch/bread

Wild Rice

. . . .

1 teaspoon canola oil
¼ cup shallots, chopped
½ cup celery, chopped
¾ cup wild rice
2½ cups Chicken Broth (see index)
2 tablespoons pine nuts (pignoli)

Combine oil with shallots and celery in a 2-cup
measure, and microwave on High for 2 minutes or
until tender. Rinse rice well, discarding any debris
that floats to surface. Drain. Place wild rice and
chicken broth in 2-quart glass measure. Microwave
on High for 5 minutes, then stir. Microwave on
Medium (60%) for 30 minutes longer. Let stand for
10 minutes, and drain off any excess liquid. When
rice is ready to serve, stir in vegetables and pine
nuts.

Variations:
1. Add cooked mushrooms and chopped parsley.
2. Substitute walnuts for pignoli.
3. Add currants and shredded part-skim mozzarella
   cheese.
4. Use half brown rice, half wild rice.

· **Serves:** 4
· **Cooking time:** 37 minutes
· **Preparation time:** 10 minutes plus standing time
· **Per Serving:** 0 Chol (mg); 26 Carbo (g); 6 Prot (g);
    467 Na (mg)
    Dietary Fiber: 2.89
    Fat (g): 4; Sat .6; Poly 1.2; Mono 1.7
    Calories: 153
    Exchanges: 2 starch/bread; 1 fat

Carbohydrates

Beans and legumes are a wonderful source of
energy. Combined with rice, a whole protein is
achieved. Combinations of peppers, onions, other
vegetables, and tomato sauces provide color, texture, and taste to the healthful bean, which
ranges from white to black, with pink, red, and
green in between.

Curried Lentils

1 tablespoon olive oil
3 shallots, minced (about ⅓ cup)
1 carrot, chopped fine
2 cloves garlic, minced
¾ cup brown (or orange) lentils
3 cups Chicken Broth, as needed (see index)
½ teaspoon fresh ginger root
1 teaspoon curry powder
2 stalks celery, chopped small
Few dashes reduced-sodium soy sauce
Few dashes sesame oil
2 tablespoons non-fat plain yogurt (optional)

In a 2-quart measure or casserole, combine olive oil, shallots, carrot, and garlic. Microwave on High for 3 minutes, stirring once, until tender. Add lentils, broth, and ginger and cover with vented plastic wrap.

Microwave on High for 30 to 35 minutes, stirring a few times. Lentils should be tender but crunchy. Drain off any excess liquid. Stir in curry powder, celery, soy, and sesame oil. Add yogurt to moisten if desired. Makes 5 cups.

- **Serves:** 10 (half-cup servings)
- **Cooking time:** 33 to 38 minutes
- **Preparation time:** 10 minutes
- **Per Serving:** 2 Chol (mg); 11 Carbo (g); 4 Prot (g); 230 Na (mg)
   Dietary Fiber: 5.8g
   Fat (g) 2; Sat .3; Poly .3; Mono .9
   Calories: 72
   Exchanges: 1 starch/bread

Green and Red Beans

½ cup celery, chopped
2 large scallions, chopped
2 cloves garlic, minced
¼ cup green pepper, chopped
½ teaspoon dried oregano
⅛ teaspoon cayenne
8 ounces kidney or pinto beans (if canned, beans should be rinsed and drained)
1 teaspoon Vogue chicken-flavored base
1 teaspoon sesame seeds

Place celery, scallions, garlic, green pepper, and spices in a 2-cup measure. Microwave on High for 5 minutes. Add beans and chicken flavoring, and microwave 1 minute on High. Stir to mix. When warmed through, toss with sesame seeds. Serve with brown rice if desired.

· Serves: 4
· Cooking time: 6 minutes
· Preparation time: 5 minutes
· Per Serving: 0 Chol (mg);   13 Carbo (g);   4 Prot (g);   225 Na (mg)
   Dietary Fiber: 3.0g
   Fat (g) 1; Sat .1; Poly .3; Mono .2
   Calories: 72
   Exchanges: 1 starch/bread

Mid-Eastern Kidney Beans

1 medium onion, chopped
1 clove garlic, minced
1 teaspoon olive oil
1 16-ounce can kidney or pinto beans,
    rinsed and drained
Juice of 1 lemon and ½ teaspoon lemon
    rind
1 teaspoon dried oregano, crushed
Pepper to taste
Few sprigs parsley for garnish
Lemon wedges for garnish

Place onion, garlic, and oil in a 4-cup measure, and microwave on High for 2 minutes. Add kidney or pinto beans, and microwave on High for 5 minutes. Mix lemon juice, lemon rind, and oregano and pepper to taste. Stir this mixture into beans and mash lightly with a fork. Garnish with parsley sprigs and lemon wedges. Serve as appetizer on bed of greens or as a side dish.

· Serves: 4
· Cooking time: 7 minutes
· Preparation time: 10 minutes
· Per Serving: 0 Chol (mg);   24 Carbo (g);   8 Prot (g);
      473 Na (mg)
      Dietary Fiber: 5.4g
      Fat (g) 2; Sat .2; Poly .4; Mono .8
      Calories: 133
      Exchanges: 1½ starch/bread

Spanish Chick Peas

1 medium onion, chopped fine
2 cloves garlic, minced
2 teaspoons olive oil
1 16-ounce can garbanzos (chick peas),
   rinsed and drained
1 medium tomato, chopped
2 tablespoons parsley, chopped
3 leaves fresh basil, or ½ teaspoon
   dried basil
Ground pepper to taste

Mix onion, garlic, and oil in a 2-quart measure, and microwave on High 2 minutes, uncovered. Add remaining ingredients, and microwave on High 4 minutes, stirring once. Serve warm or chilled. May be used as appetizer, salad or side dish.

· **Serves:** 6
· **Cooking time:** 6 minutes
· **Preparation time:** 15 minutes
· **Per Serving:** 0 Chol (mg);   13 Carbo (g);   4 Prot (g);
     259 Na (mg)
     Dietary Fiber: 4g
     Fat (g) 3;   Sat .2;   Poly .2;   Mono 1.0
     Calories: 86
     Exchanges: 1 starch/bread

Potatoes

According to Jane Brody, writing in *The New York Times,* "the potato can supply more nutritious food faster than any other foodstuff. With almost no fat, a vegetable protein that is nearly as nourishing as milk protein and a laundry list of vitamins and minerals, the potato comes close to being a perfect source of nourishment."

Potatoes lend themselves to a variety of cooking styles. The microwave bakes potatoes differently from the conventional oven: the skins will not be crisp but it only takes a few minutes. A chart for baking times, depending on the number of potatoes, is given in the recipe for Stuffed Potatoes.

Lyonnaise Potatoes

2 Idaho potatoes, about 8 ounces each, sliced thin, about ⅛-inch thick
2 medium onions, sliced thin
1 tablespoon olive oil
3 cloves garlic, minced
¼ teaspoon salt
⅛ teaspoon pepper
⅛ teaspoon paprika
1 tablespoon parsley, chopped, for garnish

Place all ingredients, except parsley, in a microwave-safe 3-quart casserole. Cover loosely with plastic wrap, and microwave on High for 12 to 14 minutes, until tender, stirring gently a few times. Garnish with parsley and let stand a few minutes before serving.

· Serves: 4
· Cooking time: 12 to 14 minutes
· Preparation time: 15 minutes
· Per Serving: 0 Chol (mg);   18 Carbo (g);   3 Prot (g);   118 Na (mg)
     Dietary Fiber: .7g
     Fat (g): 4; Sat .5; Poly .4; Mono 2.5
     Calories: 108
     Exchanges: 1 starch/bread; 1 fat

New Potato Salad

6 new potatoes, well washed
¾ cup celery, chopped (about 3 medium stalks)
¼ cup non-fat plain yogurt
1 tablespoon reduced-calorie mayonnaise
2 tablespoons tarragon vinegar
1 tablespoon Dijon mustard
1 tablespoon fresh lemon juice
1 teaspoon low-sodium soy sauce
1 tablespoon caraway seeds
Romaine or spinach leaves
Tomatoes or other fresh vegetables for garnish

Place potatoes in large glass casserole with a little water. Cover with paper towel. Microwave on High for 10 to 12 minutes, until tender but not too soft, rotating twice. Let cool and cut into quarters.

Meantime for dressing, blend together the remaining ingredients except seeds, lettuce, and garnish. Mix potatoes with dressing, toss in caraway seeds, and serve on bed of lettuce or spinach with garnish of fresh vegetables.

· **Serves:** 4
· **Cooking time:** 10 to 12 minutes
· **Preparation time:** 10 minutes
· **Per Serving:** 0 Chol (mg); 21 Carbo (g); 3 Prot (g); 155 Na (mg)
   Dietary Fiber: 3.2g
   Fat (g): 2; Sat .3; Poly .5; Mono .7
   Calories: 109
   Exchanges: 1½ starch/bread

Stuffed Potatoes

Potatoes

4 small Idaho baking potatoes, well washed but not dried. Pierce each potato once through the skin at the center. Wrap in microwave-safe paper towel, and place end-to-end in a circle on the floor of the oven. Microwave on High for 16 to 20 minutes. If baking fewer than four potatoes, follow this cooking guide:

One potato (8 ounces): 4 to 5 minutes
Two potatoes: 7 to 10 minutes
Three potatoes: 11 to 14 minutes

When potatoes are cooked, leave in paper for another minute until ready to stuff.

Yogurt Sour Cream Stuffing:

¼ cup plain Yogurt Sour Cream (see index)
2 tablespoons Parmesan or Romano cheese, grated
Chives, snipped
Dash paprika

Cut potatoes in half, lengthwise, and scoop out meat. Mix with yogurt sour cream and cheese and stuff back into shells. Top with garnish of chives and dash of paprika. Return to microwave for 1 minute on High to warm through; or, if desired, run under broiler until top browns lightly.

· **Serves:** 4
· **Cooking time:** 17 to 21 minutes
· **Preparation time:** 10 minutes
· **Per Serving:** 3 Chol (mg); 22 Carbo (g); 6 Prot (g);
    98 Na (mg)
    Dietary Fiber: 3.6g
    Fat (g): 1; Sat .6; Poly .1; Mono .2
    Calories: 116
    Exchanges: 1½ starch/bread

Turnip Yam Treat

2 medium turnips, peeled and cubed
2 medium yams, peeled and cubed
¼ cup water
¼ cup non-fat dry milk
¼ teaspoon nutmeg
Dash dried thyme
1 tablespoon frozen apple juice
   concentrate
Salt and pepper to taste

Place cubed turnips and yams in 2-quart glass measure or casserole with water. Cover with paper towel, and microwave on High for 10 to 12 minutes, stirring twice, until tender.

Turn into blender or food processor, add remaining ingredients, and puree. Return to microwave to warm for 1 minute if necessary. Season with salt and pepper. This is especially attractive if served in the center of a ring of broccoli.

· Serves: 4
· Cooking time: 11 to 13 minutes
· Preparation time: 20 minutes
· Per Serving: 1 Chol (mg);   27 Carbo (g);   3 Prot (g);
      98 Na (mg)
      Dietary Fiber: 4.4g
      Fat (g):   0;   Sat 0;   Poly 0;   Mono 0
      Calories: 116
      Exchanges: 2 starch/bread

Pasta

More and more, pasta has become the food of choice for health-conscious people. Nutritionally speaking, pasta is an ideal food. It is low in fat and cholesterol and high in complex carbohydrates, protein, B vitamins, and iron. Because it is digested slowly, it is a boon to people with diabetes since it helps maintain an even blood sugar level.

Pasta is easy to cook, versatile, and lends itself to many inventions, from the addition of fresh vegetables, seafood, or chicken to dressing with light mock cream sauces, such as a combination of part-skim ricotta and yogurt, or oriental hot sauces. The creative chef will enjoy making personal pasta dishes for the entire family. It is recommended that pasta be cooked on top of a conventional range and the sauce be cooked in the microwave oven.

Simple Pasta Preparations

- Toss hot pasta with a little freshly grated Parmesan or Romano cheese, fresh-minced garlic, and fresh pepper.

- Microwave wedges of fresh tomatoes for 1 minute and toss over pasta with minced, fresh basil and a tablespoon of olive oil.

- Rinse a can of kidney or pinto beans and heat in the microwave with a few finely chopped walnuts and a tablespoon of olive or peanut oil. Add a dash of pepper for taste.

Popular Pasta Shapes

More than 150 different pasta shapes are made in the United States. And there are even more imported from Italy. It is also possible to purchase freshly made, flavored pastas in specialty food shops, some of which are flavored with seafood, Cajun spices, or vegetables such as tomatoes and spinach. These are some of the more readily available and popular shapes:

Capellini, or Angel Hair
Conchiglie—shells, small, medium and large
Ditalini—small macaroni
Egg noodles
Elbow macaroni
Farfalle—bow ties
Fettucine—small ribbons
Fettucine verde—spinach ribbons
Fusilli—twisted spaghetti
Linguine—flat spaghetti
Orzo—small quill-shaped pasta
Penne—large quill-shaped pasta
Rigatoni—ribbed large quills

Rotelle—spiral-shaped pasta
Rotini—twists, often available in tri-color
tastes
Ruote—wheels
Spaghetti
Vermicelli—thin spaghetti strands
Ziti—large tubes, sometimes called
"bridegrooms"

Wheat-free pasta made of Jerusalem artichokes is also available and is tasteful as well as safer for those who may have wheat allergies. Spinach-flavored pasta is made by DeBoles, the same manufacturers of the wheat-free spaghetti. Buckwheat noodles (soba) are also healthful and are available in oriental and natural food stores.

Buckwheat Noodles

7 ounces soba noodles (buckwheat,
   available in natural food stores)
2 bunches scallions
1 teaspoon sesame oil
2 tablespoons reduced-sodium soy sauce
2 tablespoons water
Few dashes cayenne
1 teaspoon mustard
2 teaspoons toasted sesame seeds

Cook noodles according to package directions on conventional range top. When cooked to *al dente*, drain, turn into colander, and rinse quickly in cold water.

While noodles are cooking, trim roots and tops off scallions and slice lengthwise, then diagonally into 1-inch pieces. Place scallions in a 2-cup measure with sesame oil, and microwave on High for 1 minute. Add soy, water, cayenne, and mustard, and microwave on High another 1 minute. Turn noodles into a serving bowl, toss with sauce, and top with sesame seeds.

· **Serves:** 6
· **Cooking time:** 12 to 14 minutes
· **Preparation time:** 10 minutes
· **Per Serving:** 0 Chol (mg);   23 Carbo (g);   3 Prot (g);
     328 Na (mg)
     Dietary Fiber: 4.6g
     Fat (g):   1;   Sat .3;   Poly .8;   Mono .7
     Calories: 143
     Exchanges: 1½ starch/bread

Creamy Spinach Pasta

6 ounces spinach or whole wheat pasta
2 tablespoons Parmesan or Romano
   cheese, grated
½ cup part-skim ricotta cheese
¼ cup non-fat plain yogurt
1 tablespoon chives, chopped
2 tablespoons walnuts, chopped

Cook pasta according to package directions on conventional range top to *al dente*. Drain and keep warm.

Meantime, place remaining ingredients, except walnuts, in a blender and process until creamy. Turn into a 2-cup measure and cover with paper towel. Microwave on High for 1 to 2 minutes, stirring, just until warm. Stir into pasta and top with walnuts.

- **Serves:** 4
- **Cooking time:** 14 minutes
- **Preparation time:** 5 minutes
- **Per Serving:** 10 Chol (mg);   19 Carbo (g);   8 Prot (g);
    102 Na (mg)
    Dietary Fiber: 2.6g
    Fat (g): 4; Sat 1.9; Poly 1.0; Mono 1.1
    Calories: 140
    Exchanges: 1 starch/bread; 1 medium-fat meat

Green Noodles

6 ounces spaghetti
1 teaspoon canola oil
4 cloves garlic, peeled and smashed
1 cup scallions, sliced, green tops included
¼ cup celery leaves, chopped
½ cup Chicken Broth (see index)
2 cups greens, shredded (chicory, romaine lettuce, spinach, escarole, or a combination)
1 tomato, sliced into thin wedges
1 tablespoon toasted pumpkin seeds

Cook noodles according to package directions on conventional range top. Drain when cooked.

Meantime, place oil, garlic, and scallions in a 2-quart measure, and microwave on High for 1 minute. Add celery leaves and chicken broth, and microwave on High another 2 minutes. Add shredded greens and stir to combine; microwave on High for another 1 minute.

Stir in cooked noodles, along with tomatoes, and microwave on High for 1 minute more until warmed through. Toss with pumpkin seeds.

· Serves: 4
· Cooking time: 15 to 17 minutes
· Preparation time: 15 minutes
· Per Serving: 0 Chol (mg);   34 Carbo (g);   8 Prot (g);
    115 Na (mg)
    Dietary Fiber: 3.1g
    Fat (g): 3; Sat .4; Poly .8; Mono 1.2
    Calories: 192
    Exchanges: 2 starch/bread; 1 vegetable

Linguini with Clam Sauce

8 ounces linguini
1 teaspoon olive oil
2 onions, chopped fine
3 cloves garlic, minced
¼ teaspoon dried oregano, crushed
¼ cup sliced water chestnuts, rinsed
  and drained
1 6½-ounce can whole baby clams, drained
½ cup fresh parsley, chopped
2 tablespoons white wine or vodka
Pepper to taste

Cook linguini according to package directions on conventional range top to *al dente*. Drain in colander.

While pasta is cooking, place oil, onions, and garlic in a 4-cup measure, and microwave on High for 3 to 4 minutes, stirring once. Add oregano and water chestnuts, and microwave on High 1 minute more.

Stir in clams, parsley, and wine or vodka, and microwave on High for 1 to 2 minutes, until warmed through. When pasta is cooked and drained, toss with sauce. Season with pepper to taste.

· Serves: 6
· Cooking time: 19 minutes
· Preparation time: 20 minutes
· Per Serving: 21 Chol (mg);   34 Carbo (g);   13 Prot (g);
    39 Na (mg)
    Dietary Fiber: 2.6g
    Fat (g): 4; Sat .4; Poly .4; Mono 1.7
    Calories: 228
    Exchanges: 2 starch/bread; 1 lean meat

Pasta Pomadoro

6 ounces spaghetti or ziti
6 ounces tomato sauce
¼ cup non-fat dry milk
2 scallions, chopped
¼ cup green peas
¼ teaspoon dried basil
Pepper to taste

Cook pasta *al dente* according to package directions on conventional range top. In a bowl, mix together remaining ingredients. Cover with wax paper, and microwave on High for 2 to 3 minutes, until heated through. Stir to combine. Mix with spaghetti and serve.

· **Serves:** 4
· **Cooking time:** 12 minutes
· **Preparation time:** 5 minutes
· **Per Serving:** 1 Chol (mg);   36 Carbo (g);   7 Prot (g);
     305 Na (mg)
     Dietary Fiber: 2.0g
     Fat (g):   1;   Sat 0;   Poly 0;   Mono 0
     Calories: 177
     Exchanges: 2 starch/bread;   1 vegetable

Pignoli and Tomato Orzo

1 teaspoon olive oil
1 tablespoon pine nuts (pignoli)
¼ cup sun-dried tomatoes
Salt and pepper to taste
2 cups Chicken Broth (see index)
2 cups water
¾ cup orzo (small quill-shaped pasta)
1 tablespoon Romano or Parmesan
   cheese, grated

Soak dried tomatoes in boiling water until soft; drain and dice. Place pine nuts and tomatoes in a measuring cup with the oil. Microwave on High for 2 minutes, and season with salt and pepper. Let stand.

Bring the chicken broth and water to a boil by microwaving on High for about 5 minutes. Add orzo and microwave on High for 6 to 8 minutes, until tender. Drain and mix with pine nuts and tomatoes. Stir in grated cheese.

- Serves: 4
- Cooking time: 13 to 15 minutes
- Preparation time: 10 minutes
- Per Serving: 2 Chol (mg); 20 Carbo (g); 7 Prot (g); 65 Na (mg)
  Dietary Fiber: 1g
  Fat (g): 6; Sat 1.0; Poly 1.7; Mono 2.3
  Calories: 151
  Exchanges: 1 starch/bread; 1 fat

Red and Yellow Pepper Pasta

6 ounces pasta (shells, rotelles, or angel hair)
1 pound red and yellow bell peppers, seeded and chopped (4 cups)
2 cloves garlic, minced
1 small red onion, quartered and sliced
1 teaspoon olive oil
2 tablespoons tomato paste diluted with ½ cup water
2 tablespoons chopped fresh basil or 1 teaspoon dried basil
2 tablespoons balsamic vinegar
Dash salt and pepper

Cook pasta according to package directions to *al dente* on conventional range top, drain, and keep warm.

Meantime, place peppers, garlic, onion, and olive oil in a 1-quart measure or casserole and microwave on High for 2 to 3 minutes, until tender. Stir.

Add tomato paste, basil and enough water to make a sauce, and vinegar. Microwave another 1 minute on High to warm. Combine with pasta and season with salt and pepper to taste.

· **Serves:** 4
· **Cooking time:** 15 to 16 minutes
· **Preparation time:** 10 minutes
· **Per Serving:** 0 Chol (mg); 25 Carbo (g); 5 Prot (g); 105 Na (mg)
   Dietary Fiber: 5.6g
   Fat (g): 2; Sat .3; Poly .5; Mono .8
   Calories: 125
   Exchanges: 1 starch/bread; 2 vegetables

Vegetable-Sauced Rotelles

10 ounces dry rotelles (spirals),
   tomato and spinach flavored
½ Red onion, chopped
1 medium green pepper, chopped
2 cloves garlic, minced
4 mushrooms, sliced
1 teaspoon olive oil
¼ teaspoon oregano
¼ to ½ teaspoon red pepper flakes
10 ounces tomato sauce
2 tablespoons part-skim mozzarella, shredded

Cook pasta *al dente*, according to package directions. Drain and set aside.

Mix next four ingredients with olive oil in a 2-quart casserole, and microwave on High for 3 minutes. Add remaining ingredients, except cheese, cover with vented plastic wrap, and microwave on High for another 1 minute, until warm.

Mix in pasta and sprinkle with cheese. Microwave uncovered for about 40 seconds to 1 minute, until cheese is melted.

· **Serves:** 6
· **Cooking time:** 16 minutes
· **Preparation time:** 15 minutes
· **Per Serving:** 3 Chol (mg);   42 Carbo (g);   10 Prot (g);
      354 Na (mg)
   Dietary Fiber: 7g
   Fat (g): 3; Sat .7; Poly .2; Mono .8
   Calories: 226
   Exchanges: 3 starch/bread; ½ fat

Vegetables

Mom was probably right to tell you to eat your
spinach. She might well have just suggested the
great span of fresh vegetables that are now available year round. Many of the recipes for leafy
green vegetables—very high in calcium—can be in-
terchanged: collards, mustard greens, kale, spinach, all may be made in similar ways. Carrots,
fennel, beans, squash, cabbage, and turnips are
all high in fiber and rich in nutrients. The addition to vegetables dishes of fresh herbs and spices
as well as seeds and nuts provides more color,
taste, and texture.

    The microwave oven is a boon to vegetables;
they are so quick to cook that none of the
nutrients are lost, as in long cooking, and very little extra liquid is needed for their preparation. It
is also a time-saver to cook the vegetables right in
the very dishes you will use to serve them. No
more pots to scrub!

When shopping for vegetables, select only brightly colored and unwilted greens and fresh, sturdy carrots, zucchini, peppers, fennel, and beans. Leafy green vegetables should be washed in tepid water to rid them of sand, then run under cold water. Any discolored leaves should be discarded.

While frozen vegetables are, in general, less desirable than fresh produce, some flash-frozen foods triumph, such as green peas and corn niblets. These need only to be taken from the freezer and added to the recipe, as they will thaw in the cooking.

Acorn Squash

2 acorn squash, about 1¼ pounds each
   (buttercup or butternut squash may
   also be used)
2 tablespoons non-fat plain yogurt
Cinnamon
Nutmeg
Mace
Black pepper
8 pecan halves, chopped

Pierce sides of each squash with fork. Wrap each in microwave-safe paper towel. Microwave on High for 5 minutes, turn, and microwave on High another 5 minutes. Remove paper, cut squash in half and remove seeds and tough pulp. Place dollop of yogurt in each center, and sprinkle with a few dashes of the spices. Top with chopped pecans.

· **Serves:** 4
· **Cooking time:** 10 minutes
· **Preparation time:** 5 minutes
· **Per Serving:** 0 Chol (mg);   16 Carbo (g);   2 Prot (g);
      10 Na (mg)
     Dietary Fiber: 5.2g
     Fat (g): 2; Sat .2; Poly .6; Mono 1.4
     Calories: 84
     Exchanges: 1 starch/bread

Bok Choy

· ·

1 pound bok choy (Chinese celery),
about 6 cups
1 teaspoon reduced-sodium soy sauce
1 clove garlic, minced
1 tablespoon frozen apple juice
concentrate
½ teaspoon sesame oil
Dash ground ginger
1 tablespoon roasted pumpkin seeds

Chop bok choy into 1-inch slices and shred tops.
Combine with remaining ingredients, except pumpkin seeds, and place in 2-quart glass measure or
baking dish. Cover with vented plastic wrap, and
microwave on High for 3 to 4 minutes, stirring
once. Drain, toss with pumpkin seeds, and serve.

· Serves: 4
· **Cooking time:** 3 to 4 minutes
· **Preparation time:** 8 minutes
· **Per Serving:** 0 Chol (mg);   6 Carbo (g);   5 Prot (g);
133 Na (mg)
Dietary Fiber: 7.3g
Fat (g): 2; Sat .4; Poly 1.1; Mono .7
Calories: 58
Exchanges: 1 vegetable

Brussels Sprouts Almandine

1 pound Brussels sprouts, cut in half
¼ cup Chicken Broth (see index)
1 clove garlic, minced
1 teaspoon whipped butter
1 teaspoon grainy Dijon mustard
1 tablespoon lemon juice
Dash pepper
¼ cup blanched almonds, slivered

Discard any discolored outer leaves, and rinse Brussels sprouts. Place in 1-quart casserole or serving dish with chicken broth. Cover with wax paper and microwave on High for 3 to 4 minutes, stir, and microwave on High for another 3 to 4 minutes. Remove from oven and let rest a minute or two.

Meantime, combine remaining ingredients, and microwave on High for 40 seconds. Drain sprouts and toss with warmed sauce.

· **Serves:** 4
· **Cooking time:** 7 to 9 minutes
· **Preparation time:** 10 minutes
· **Per Serving:** 0 Chol (mg); 9 Carbo (g); 3 Prot (g);
        86 Na (mg)
     Dietary Fiber: 4.3g
     Fat (g): 4; Sat .5; Poly 1.0; Mono 2.1
     Calories: 68
     Exchanges: 2 vegetable; 1 fat

Caraway Cabbage

1 head green cabbage, about 1 to 1¼ pounds
2 tablespoons frozen apple juice concentrate
2 tablespoons grainy Dijon mustard
4 drops sesame oil
1½ tablespoons caraway seeds

Trim stem off cabbage and cut into 8 wedges. Mix together remaining ingredients. Arrange cabbage wedges on their sides on a 12-inch glass baking dish, and coat with mustard mixture. Cover with vented plastic wrap, and microwave on High for 5 to 6 minutes. Rotate dish and microwave on High another 5 to 6 minutes, until crisp tender.

- Serves: 4
- Cooking time: 10 to 12 minutes
- Preparation time: 8 minutes
- Per Serving: 0 Chol (mg);   7 Carbo (g);   1 Prot (g);   107 Na (mg)
  Dietary Fiber: 1.6g
  Fat (g): .1; Sat 0; Poly 0; Mono 0
  Calories: 34
  Exchanges: 1 vegetable

Pimento Asparagus

1¼ pounds fresh asparagus
2 tablespoons fresh lemon juice
2 tablespoons pimentos, chopped
1 tablespoon toasted pine nuts
(pignoli)

Snap ends off asparagus and rinse. Arrange on platter in single layer. Drizzle on lemon juice, and sprinkle pimento pieces on top. Cover with wax paper.

Microwave on High for 5 to 6 minutes, turning dish once during cycle. Cook another 1 minute or so if softer spears are desired. Toss pine nuts over asparagus and serve.

· **Serves:** 4
· **Cooking time:** 6 to 7 minutes
· **Preparation time:** 5 minutes
· **Per Serving:** 0 Chol (mg); 7 Carbo (g); 3 Prot (g);
   6 Na (mg)
   Dietary Fiber: 3.5g
   Fat (g): 2; Sat .3; Poly .7; Mono .5
   Calories: 37
   Exchanges: 1 vegetable

Pine Nut Green Beans

1 pound fresh green beans, trimmed
and washed
½ cup Italian plum tomatoes, drained
and crushed
2 tablespoons toasted pine nuts
(pignoli)
Dash pepper

Place green beans and tomatoes in an 8-inch baking
dish or casserole and stir to mix. Cover with lid or
wax paper. Microwave on High for 7 to 9 minutes
or until tender, stirring twice. Drain off any excess
liquid, toss with pine nuts, and season with pepper.

· Serves: 4
· Cooking time: 7 to 9 minutes
· Preparation time: 10 minutes
· Per Serving: 0 Chol (mg); 7 Carbo (g); 3 Prot (g);
      51 Na (mg)
   Dietary Fiber: 2.3g
   Fat (g): 3; Sat .4; Poly 1.2; Mono 1.0
   Calories: 53
   Exchanges: 1 vegetable; ½ fat

Ratatouille

. . . .

1 small eggplant, cubed
1 onion, chopped
6 cloves garlic, peeled and
   smashed
1 tablespoon olive oil
2 cups tomatoes, cubed (cherry
   tomatoes, halved, are fine)
1 medium zucchini or yellow
   squash, sliced
2 tablespoons chopped fresh basil
   or ½ teaspoon dried basil
1 teaspoon dried thyme
1 teaspoon dried oregano
Salt and pepper to taste
1 medium red bell pepper, cut into
   1-inch squares
1 medium green or yellow bell
   pepper, cut into 1-inch squares
½ to 1 teaspoon hot red pepper flakes

In a 2-quart measure or casserole, place eggplant, onion, garlic, and oil. Microwave on High for 10 minutes, stirring once or twice. Add tomatoes, zucchini, and spices and microwave on High 10

(Please turn page)

minutes, stirring once. Add peppers and hot pepper
flakes and microwave another 5 minutes on High.
Stir to blend. Let rest before serving warm or
chilled.

· **Serves:** 8
· **Cooking time:** 25 minutes
· **Preparation time:** 15 to 20 minutes
· **Per Serving:** 0 Chol (mg); 8 Carbo (g); 1 Prot (g);
    21 Na (mg)
    Dietary Fiber: 2.5g
    Fat (g): 2; Sat .3; Poly .3; Mono 1.3
    Calories: 48
    Exchanges: 1 vegetable

Ruby Red Cabbage

1 medium onion
4 cloves garlic, peeled and minced
2 teaspoons canola oil
¾ pound red cabbage, shredded (about 4 cups)
¼ cup balsamic vinegar
2 tablespoons frozen orange juice concentrate
1 cup Chicken Broth (see index)
3 tablespoons raisins
1 tablespoon ginger root, chopped fine
½ teaspoon cloves, powdered
1 bay leaf
Juice of 1 lemon

Place onion, garlic, and oil in 2-quart casserole or measuring cup, and microwave on High for 3 minutes. Mix with shredded cabbage and remaining ingredients, cover with wax paper, and microwave on High for 4 minutes. Stir, and microwave on High for another 4 minutes. When cabbage is tender, discard bay leaf.

· **Serves:** 6
· **Cooking time:** 11 minutes
· **Preparation time:** 15 minutes
· **Per Serving:** 1 Chol (mg);   9 Carbo (g);   2 Prot (g);   193 Na (mg)
    Dietary Fiber: 3.8g
    Fat (g):   3;   Sat .6;   Poly 1.8;   Mono .9
    Calories: 99
    Exchanges: 2 vegetable

Rutabaga Mousse

1 rutabaga, about 1¼ pounds
½ cup water
⅛ teaspoon nutmeg, grated
¼ teaspoon cinnamon, ground
½ teaspoon celery seed
4 tablespoons non-fat dry milk
1 tablespoon part-skim ricotta cheese
¼ cup frozen apple juice concentrate
2 tablespoons parsley, chopped

Peel and dice rutabaga and place in 2-quart measure with water. Cover with vented plastic wrap, and microwave on High for 20 minutes, until tender. Turn into food processor, reserving some cooking liquid if needed later to thin.

Add all remaining ingredients, except parsley, and process to blend. Microwave on High for 30 to 40 seconds, until warm. Garnish with parsley.

· Serves: 6
· Cooking time: 21 minutes
· Preparation time: 10 minutes
· Per Serving: 2 Chol (mg);   9 Carbo (g);   3 Prot (g);
     49 Na (mg)
     Dietary Fiber: 1.7g
     Fat (g):   1;   Sat .2;   Poly .1;   Mono .1
     Calories: 69
     Exchanges: 2 vegetable

Sesame Spinach

. . . .

1 teaspoon sesame oil
2 cloves garlic, minced
½ onion, chopped
1½ pounds fresh spinach
1 teaspoon reduced-sodium soy sauce
⅛ teaspoon fresh ginger root, minced
2 tablespoons sliced water chestnuts,
    rinsed and drained
2 teaspoons toasted sesame seeds

Place oil in measuring cup with garlic and onion, and microwave on High for 1 minute, until tender. Wash spinach well and cut off tough stems; place it in 4-quart casserole with just the water left on the leaves. Cover with vented plastic wrap, and microwave on High for 4 to 6 minutes, stirring once, until wilted.

Drain spinach, mix with onion and garlic mixture, add soy, ginger root, and water chestnuts, and microwave on High 1 more minute. Toss with sesame seeds and serve. This is also nice as a salad if served chilled.

· Serves: 4
· **Cooking time:** 6 to 8 minutes
· **Preparation time:** 10 minutes
· **Per Serving:** 0 Chol (mg);   9 Carbo (g);   6 Prot (g);
    189 Na (mg)
    Dietary Fiber: 1.4g
    Fat (g):   3;   Sat .4;   Poly 1.0;   Mono .8
    Calories: 65
    Exchanges: 2 vegetable; ½ fat

Sesame Eggplant

1 medium eggplant, about 1½ pounds
2 stalks fresh asparagus (or 1 cup broccoli)
3 tablespoons carrot, chopped
½ teaspoon dried basil
2 cloves garlic, peeled
1 tablespoon olive oil
½ teaspoon sesame oil
1 tablespoon toasted sesame seeds
Salt and pepper to taste

Peel eggplant and chop into 1-inch pieces. Cut asparagus or broccoli into small pieces. Combine all ingredients, except sesame seeds and salt and pepper. Place in large bowl and cover with wax paper.

Microwave on High for 2 to 3 minutes. Turn bowl and stir. Microwave on High another 2 to 3 minutes. Stir, adding sesame seeds and seasoning.

· Serves: 4
· Cooking time: 4 to 6 minutes
· Preparation time: 20 minutes
· Per Serving: 0 Chol (mg); 11 Carbo (g); 4 Prot (g);
    15 Na (mg)
    Dietary Fiber: 3.9g
    Fat (g): 5; Sat .8; Poly 1.2; Mono 3.2
    Calories: 95
    Exchanges: 2 vegetable; 1 fat

Any combination of vegetables may be substituted, according to availability or choice. Use zucchini or summer squash slices, asparagus, turnips, wax or green beans. Always place softer vegetables in center of arrangement.

· **Serves:** 4
· **Cooking time:** 3 to 5 minutes
· **Preparation time:** 15 minutes
· **Per Serving:** 0 Chol (mg);   11 Carbo (g);   5 Prot (g);
         20 Na (mg)
      Dietary Fiber: 4.9g
      Fat (g):   0;   Sat 0;   Poly 0;   Mono 0
      Calories: 57
      Exchanges: 2 vegetable

Sauces

Sauces add a little something extra to nearly everything. Depending upon your tastes, they may be used to top grains or pasta, potatoes, vegetables, poultry, fish, or even desserts. Some sauces may also be used as dips for pre-meal teasers. Inventive cooks can combine whatever they like, using non-fat milk or yogurt or low-fat cottage cheese, tomato and vegetable combinations pureed, and even peanut butter or nuts. Experimenting and experiencing taste treats are fun.

Caper Sauce

¼ cup non-fat plain yogurt
1 tablespoon capers, rinsed and drained
1 teaspoon Dijon mustard
2 teaspoons parsley, chopped
⅛ teaspoon paprika
⅛ teaspoon pepper

Combine all ingredients in 1-cup measure, and microwave on High for 30 seconds to 1 minute, just until warm. Spoon over poached fish, such as salmon, or poultry.

· **Serves:** 4 (2-tablespoon servings)
· **Cooking time:** 1 minute
· **Preparation time:** 2 minutes
· **Per Serving:** 0 Chol (mg); 1 Carbo (g); 1 Prot (g);
    27 Na (mg)
    Dietary Fiber: 0g
    Fat (g): 0; Sat 0; Poly 0; Mono 0
    Calories: 7
    Exchanges: free

Cranberry and Orange Sauce

1 12-ounce package fresh cranberries
¼ cup frozen orange juice concentrate
1 orange
2 tablespoons walnuts, chopped

Wash cranberries and discard any debris. Combine in a 1-quart casserole or measure with orange juice. Cover with vented plastic wrap, and microwave on High 5 minutes, until soft. Cut the orange into quarters, then eighths.

Let cranberries cool a bit before turning half of them into a food processor with half of the orange sections. Puree, and pour into serving bowl. Process remaining cranberries and oranges and add to serving bowl. Chill before serving, and garnish with chopped walnuts. Makes 2 cups.

· **Serves:** 16 (2-tablespoon servings)
· **Cooking time:** 5 minutes
· **Preparation time:** 7 minutes
· **Per Serving:** 0 Chol (mg);   5 Carbo (g);   0 Prot (g);
    0 Na (mg)
    Dietary Fiber: 1.0g
    Fat (g): 0; Sat 0; Poly 0; Mono 0
    Calories: 21
    Exchanges: free

Lemon Sauce

1 lemon, washed, trimmed, and cut
    into pieces
1 cup soft tofu (bean curd)
Few dashes sesame oil
¼ cup non-fat plain yogurt
1 teaspoon horseradish
1 teaspoon Dijon mustard
¼ teaspoon salt
Fresh pepper to taste
1 teaspoon black olives, chopped
    (optional)

Blend all ingredients, except olives, in a food processor and turn into a 4-cup measure. Microwave on High for 2 minutes, stirring once. Top with chopped olives if desired. Serve over pasta, grains, or fish or use as an appetizer dip with crudités. It's even good served on a dessert! Makes 2 cups.

· **Serves:** 16 (2-tablespoon servings)
· **Cooking time:** 2 minutes
· **Preparation time:** 5 minutes
· **Per Serving:** 0 Chol (mg); 0 Carbo (g); 1 Prot (g);
      20 Na (mg)
      Dietary Fiber: 0g
      Fat (g): 0; Sat .1; Poly .2; Mono .1
      Calories: 6
      Exchanges: free

Saucy Salsa

3 cloves garlic, minced
½ cup onion, chopped
4 ounces tomato puree
4 ounces fresh ripe tomatoes, chopped,
   or canned Italian plum tomatoes,
   drained and crushed
1 fresh green chili, chopped
½ teaspoon ground cumin
½ teaspoon dried oregano

Place garlic and onion in 1-quart glass measure, and microwave on High for 1½ to 2 minutes. Add remaining ingredients and cover with plastic wrap. Microwave on High for 2 to 3 minutes and stir to blend.

· **Serves:** 4 (as sauce)
· **Cooking time:** 3½ to 5 minutes
· **Preparation time:** 10 minutes
· **Per Serving:** 0 Chol (mg);   6 Carbo (g);   1 Prot (g);
      128 Na (mg)
      Dietary Fiber: .8g
      Fat (g):   0;   Sat 0;   Poly 0;   Mono 0
      Calories: 27
      Exchanges: 1 vegetable

Spinach Sauce

½ pound fresh spinach, trimmed of
  tough stems, well washed
½ tablespoon olive oil
1 tablespoon oat bran
Pepper to taste
⅛ teaspoon ground nutmeg
¼ teaspoon ground cardamom
1 tablespoon lemon juice
½ cup non-fat plain yogurt at room
  temperature

Place wet spinach in a 2-quart casserole or mea-sure, and microwave on High for 1 to 2 minutes, until wilted. Puree in food processor or blender with all remaining ingredients except yogurt.

Return to casserole and microwave on High for another 1 minute, stirring. Blend in yogurt and ad-just seasoning. Serve over fish, poultry, pasta, or rice or use as an appetizer dip.

· **Serves:** 12 (2-tablespoon servings)
· **Cooking time:** 2 to 3 minutes
· **Preparation time:** 10 minutes
· **Per Serving:** 1 Chol (mg); 4 Carbo (g); 3 Prot (g);
    70 Na (mg)
    Dietary Fiber: 1.7g
    Fat (g): 2; Sat .3; Poly .2; Mono 1.3
    Calories: 40
    Exchanges: 1 vegetable

Walnut Sauce

½ cup walnuts or pecans, shelled
1 teaspoon Dijon mustard
1 teaspoon olive oil
2 to 3 tablespoons fresh lemon juice
1 teaspoon whole wheat bread
crumbs
1 tablespoon frozen apple juice
concentrate

Chop nuts in food processor, then add remaining ingredients and puree. Place in 2-cup measure, and microwave on High for 1 to 2 minutes to warm through. Serve over fish or poultry or even pasta or potatoes. This sauce is also tasty enough to be used as an appetizer, spreading a little on an endive leaf or cracker.

· **Serves:** 5 (2-tablespoon servings)
· **Cooking time:** 1 to 2 minutes
· **Preparation time:** 5 minutes
· **Per Serving:** 0 Chol (mg);   4 Carbo (g);   1 Prot (g);
    17 Na (mg)
    Dietary Fiber: .9g
    Fat (g):   8;   Sat .7;   Poly 1.8;   Mono 5
    Calories: 99
    Exchanges: 2 fat

Yogurt Sour Cream

2 cups non-fat plain yogurt
Flavors as desired (see below)

Place yogurt in a cheesecloth or coffee-filter-lined sieve, and let drip over a bowl in the refrigerator for 4 to 6 hours or overnight, until the yogurt has the consistency of thick sour cream. Makes 1 cup.

Flavored Yogurt Sour Cream: For a sweet flavor, add cinnamon, vanilla extract, or frozen orange juice concentrate. For savory tastes, add herbs such as dill, tarragon, parsley, oregano, or caraway before placing yogurt in sieve.

· **Serves:** 16 (1-tablespoon servings)
· **Cooking time:** 0
· **Preparation time:** 2 minutes plus refrigerating time
· **Per Serving:** 1 Chol (mg); 3 Carbo (g); 2 Prot (g);
     0 Na (mg)
     Dietary Fiber: 0g
     Fat (g): 0; Sat 0; Poly 0; Mono 0
     Calories: 22
     Exchanges: free

Baked Goods

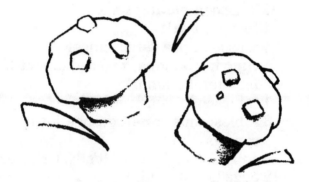

Everything I had read told me that you just can't bake in a microwave oven. Wrong! Much to my delight, I discovered that you can bake quickly and efficiently in a microwave. I tried some of my favorite breads and muffins and found that they came out just as tasteful and in less time than when using a conventional oven. The baked goods do not have a browned top, but that is readily overcome by dusting the top with poppy or caraway seeds or paprika and running them under the conventional broiler for a few seconds. The results are well worth the paler look.

Banana Bread

· · · · · · · · · · · · · · · · · · · ·

Non-stick vegetable spray
1½ cups all-purpose unbleached flour
¼ cup rye flour
1½ teaspoons baking powder
½ teaspoon baking soda
¼ teaspoon salt
½ teaspoon powdered ginger
1 cup ripe banana, mashed (about 2
   medium bananas)
1 tablespoon lemon juice
3 tablespoons frozen orange juice
   concentrate
⅓ cup I Can't Believe It's Not Butter
2 eggs (1 yolk only)
⅓ cup evaporated skim milk
½ cup pecans or walnuts, chopped
2 tablespoons plus 1 teaspoon
   currants
Few dashes cinnamon

Coat the bottom of a 9 x 5-inch glass loaf pan with
non-stick vegetable spray. In a bowl, mix together
the flours, baking powder, baking soda, salt, and
ginger. In another small bowl, mash bananas, mix
with lemon juice, and set aside.

In a large bowl, combine the orange juice, I
Can't Believe It's Not Butter, eggs, and milk. Stir in
chopped nuts and 2 tablespoons currants. Fold in
mashed bananas and add dry ingredients, mixing
well. Turn into baking dish and top with 1 teaspoon
currants and a few dashes of cinnamon.

Place in microwave oven on inverted saucer. Microwave on Medium-High (70%) for 3½ to 4 minutes. Turn pan and continue microwaving at 70% for another 3½ to 4 minutes. Microwave on High for 4 to 5 minutes, until a knife inserted into the center of the bread comes out clean.

If a browned top is desired, place under conventional oven broiler for 30 seconds. Let cool 10 minutes. Remove from pan. If bottom is still damp, return to microwave, bottom up, and microwave on High for 1 to 2 minutes, until no longer wet.

This bread gets better after refrigeration for a day (if it's not all eaten!).

- **Serves:** 12 (1 slice each)
- **Cooking time:** 12–15 minutes
- **Preparation time:** 30 minutes plus cooling time
- **Per Serving:** 23 Chol (mg);   23 Carbo (g);   4 Prot (g);   169 Na (mg)
    Dietary Fiber: 1.8g
    Fat (g): 6;   Sat 1;   Poly 1.7;   Mono 3.3
    Calories: 161
    Exchanges: 1½ starch/bread;   1 fat

Blueberry Cobbler

2 cups fresh blueberries
⅓ cup whole wheat flour
⅓ cup unbleached all-purpose flour
1 teaspoon baking soda
3 tablespoons frozen orange juice
    concentrate
1 cup non-fat plain yogurt
1 teaspoon poppy seeds

Wash blueberries and pick over, discarding any debris. Turn into an 8-inch-square baking dish.

Mix together the flours and baking soda. Stir in orange juice and yogurt and when blended, pour over berries. Sprinkle poppy seeds over dough and place in oven on an inverted saucer.

Microwave on High for 4 to 5 minutes. Rotate dish and microwave on High another 4 to 5 minutes. Cobbler is done when it springs back when touched lightly. Top with blend of cottage cheese and part-skim ricotta if desired.

· **Serves:** 8
· **Cooking time:** 8 to 10 minutes
· **Preparation time:** 15 minutes
· **Per Serving:** 1 Chol (mg);   15 Carbo (g);   3 Prot (g);
    127 Na (mg)
    Dietary Fiber: 1.8g
    Fat (g):   0;   Sat 0;   Poly 0;   Mono 0
    Calories: 72
    Exchanges: 1 starch/bread

Desserts

I have always had a preference for a simple piece of fruit to finish off a good meal. But many people crave something more elaborate as a dessert, particularly when other people without diabetes share a meal. The microwave does a good job of whipping up delectable desserts in short order. Many of these recipes are fruit-based, and many use low-fat milk or yogurt and even grains and potatoes.

Fruit is the natural sweetener in all the recipes, so fear of too much sugar is never an issue.

To have berries or melon on hand when they are not in season, try freezing them on a cookie sheet and then storing them in small quantities in plastic freezer bags. Blackberries, strawberries, raspberries, and blueberries may all be kept frozen and used to make dessert dressings or toppings throughout the year. Melon may be scooped into small rounds or cut into chunks and frozen in the same way.

Apricot Prune Whip

· ·

½ cup water
½ cup dried apricots
½ cup prunes, pitted
1 cup soft tofu (bean curd)
2 teaspoons pure vanilla extract
2 tablespoons non-fat dry milk
4 medium strawberries (or raspberries)

Place water, apricots, and prunes in 2-cup glass measure, and microwave on High for 2 to 3 minutes, until soft. Let cool. Place fruit in food processor with remaining ingredients, except berries, and whip until smooth. Serve warm or chilled, topped with strawberries for garnish.

· Serves: 4
· Cooking time: 2 to 3 minutes
· Preparation time: 5 minutes
· Per Serving: 0 Chol (mg); 17 Carbo (g); 6 Prot (g);
    18 Na (mg)
    Dietary Fiber: 4.7g
    Fat (g): 3; Sat .5; Poly 1.6; Mono .7
    Calories: 110
    Exchanges: 1 fruit; 1 lean meat

Bette's Baked Apples

4 McIntosh apples, cored
2 tablespoons raisins
2 tablespoons sunflower seeds
2 teaspoons powdered cinnamon
2 tablespoons frozen apple juice
    concentrate
1 tablespoon water

Peel away about ½ inch of skin from top of apples and pierce with a fork in several places. Fill cores with raisins, sunflower seeds, a few dashes of cinnamon, and a dab of apple juice. Place in deep baking dish, add water, and cover with vented plastic wrap. Microwave on High for 5 to 6 minutes, turning dish once. Spoon sauce over apples and serve warm or chilled.

· **Serves:** 4
· **Cooking time:** 5 to 6 minutes
· **Preparation time:** 10 minutes
· **Per Serving:** 0 Chol (mg);   23 Carbo (g);   1 Prot (g);   2 Na (mg)
    Dietary Fiber: 2.5g
    Fat (g): 2;   Sat .3;   Poly 1.4;   Mono .4
    Calories: 109
    Exchanges: 1½ fruit

Buttercup Cream

1 buttercup or butternut squash, about
   1¼ pounds
2 tablespoons part-skim ricotta cheese
2 tablespoons non-fat dry milk
1 tablespoon frozen orange juice
   concentrate
Dash cinnamon
Dash nutmeg
1 tablespoon almonds, slivered

Pierce squash with a fork in several places. Arrange over two layers of microwave-safe paper towels, and microwave on High for 4 to 5 minutes, turning once. When soft, cut in half, discard seeds, and scoop out flesh. Let cool in refrigerator, then mix with all remaining ingredients, except almonds, in blender or food processor. Blend and serve in parfait glasses, topped with almonds.

Note: acorn or butternut squash may also be used for this dish.

· **Serves:** 4
· **Cooking time:** 4 to 5 minutes
· **Preparation time:** 10 minutes plus cooling time
· **Per Serving:** 23 Chol (mg);   16 Carbo (g);   3 Prot (g);
      25 Na (mg)
   Dietary Fiber: 4.5g
   Fat (g):   1;   Sat .4;   Poly .2;   Mono .6
   Calories: 80
   Exchanges: 1 starch/bread

Cool Carob Pudding

¼ cup unsweetened carob powder (or cocoa)
2 cups evaporated skim milk
1 teaspoon pure vanilla extract
1 teaspoon instant coffee (decaf optional)
1 teaspoon frozen orange juice concentrate
Filberts, chopped

Combine all ingredients, except nuts, in blender and turn into a 4-cup measure. Cover tightly with vented plastic wrap, and microwave on High for 3 to 4 minutes. Place in freezer for about 1 hour before serving. Stir with fork, spoon into dessert dishes, and top with sprinkle of nuts.

· **Serves:** 4
· **Cooking time:** 3 to 4 minutes
· **Preparation time:** 5 minutes plus cooling time
· **Per Serving:** 5 Chol (mg);   18 Carbo (g);   11 Prot (g);   148 Na (mg)
  Dietary Fiber: .4g
  Fat (g): 2;   Sat .9;   Poly .8;   Mono .4
  Calories: 126
  Exchanges: 1½ skim milk

Corn and Peanut Pudding

¾ cup canned or frozen corn niblets
1 cup skim milk
1 heaping teaspoon oat bran
1 tablespoon unsweetened coconut, shredded and divided
2 tablespoons frozen orange juice concentrate
1 teaspoon pure vanilla extract
1 teaspoon maple extract
¼ teaspoon ground allspice
½ teaspoon ground ginger
1 tablespoon crunchy peanut butter (no sugar added)
2 tablespoons unsalted peanuts, chopped
Carob chips, unsweetened (available in health food stores)

Microwave corn with liquid on High for 3 minutes. Drain. Turn corn niblets into food processor and puree. Pour in milk and all remaining ingredients except peanuts, carob chips, and half tablespoon of the coconut. Process until smooth.

Pour into 8-inch deep casserole, and microwave uncovered on High for 3 minutes. Stir, and microwave another 1 to 2 minutes, until thick. Let rest a few minutes and top with remaining coconut, peanuts, and carob chips. Serve warm or chilled.

- **Serves:** 4
- **Cooking time:** 7 to 8 minutes
- **Preparation time:** 10 minutes
- **Per Serving:** 1 Chol (mg);   14 Carbo (g);   5 Prot (g);   56 Na (mg)
    Dietary Fiber: 2.2g
    Fat (g):   4;   Sat 1.0;   Poly 1.0;   Mono 1.6
    Calories: 103
    Exchanges: 1 starch/bread;   1 fat

Couscous Pudding

· ·

2 cups skim milk
¾ cup couscous
1 tablespoon currants
½ teaspoon orange zest
½ teaspoon whipped butter
2 teaspoons pure vanilla extract
1 tablespoon almonds, chopped
Few dashes cinnamon
2 strawberries, sliced in half

Pour milk into 6-cup glass measure or casserole, and microwave on High for 2 to 3 minutes, until it boils. Add couscous and remaining ingredients, except almonds, cinnamon and strawberries. Microwave on High for 4 to 5 minutes, until liquid is absorbed. Stir to blend.

Let rest 5 minutes. Spoon into individual dessert glasses, and top with almonds and dash of cinnamon. Garnish with strawberry slice.

· **Serves:** 4
· **Cooking time:** 6 to 8 minutes
· **Preparation time:** 5 minutes plus resting time
· **Per Serving:** 3 Chol (mg);   22 Carbo (g);   8 Prot (g);   73 Na (mg)
    Dietary Fiber: .7g
    Fat (g):   2;   Sat .4;   Poly .2;   Mono .6
    Calories: 132
    Exchanges: 1 starch/bread;   ½ skim milk

Crême Fraiche

1 cup part-skim ricotta cheese
¼ cup buttermilk

Whip cheese and buttermilk in blender until smooth. Pour into dish and microwave on High 1 to 2 minutes, until just warm. Let stand a few hours before chilling. Use a dollop over fruit desserts.

· **Serves:** 10 (2-tablespoon servings)
· **Cooking time:** 1 to 2 minutes
· **Preparation time:** 2 minutes plus standing and chilling time
· **Per Serving:** 7 Chol (mg);   1 Carbo (g);   3 Prot (g);   32 Na (mg)
    Dietary Fiber: 0g
    Fat (g):   2;   Sat 1.1;   Poly .1;   Mono .5
    Calories: 31
    Exchanges: free (limit to 2-tablespoon serving)

Fancy Fruit Soup

½ cup dried apricots
½ cup Dole's orange-pineapple-banana
   juice (or orange juice)
½ cup prunes, pitted
1 cinnamon stick
4 whole cloves
2 slices lemon
2 tablespoons non-fat plain yogurt
1 tablespoon pecans, chopped
1 teaspoon unsweetened coconut

Place apricots in medium bowl with ½ cup juice and cover with vented plastic wrap. Microwave on High for 1 minute. Add prunes, cinnamon stick, cloves, and lemon and microwave on High for another 2 minutes, until fruit is soft. Remove cloves and cinnamon stick, mix in yogurt, and serve with sprinkling of pecans and coconut if desired. This is even better after chilling overnight.

· **Serves:** 4
· **Cooking time:** 3 minutes
· **Preparation time:** 5 minutes
· **Per Serving:** 0 Chol (mg); 19 Carbo (g); 1 Prot (g);
   9 Na (mg)
   Dietary Fiber: 4.7g
   Fat (g): 1; Sat .2; Poly .2; Mono .4
   Calories: 81
   Exchanges: 1 fruit

Indonesian Pudding

1 yam (about ¼ pound), peeled
   and cut into small cubes
2 tablespoons frozen orange juice
   concentrate
1 cinnamon stick
1½ to 2 ripe bananas, peeled and sliced
   (about 1 cup)
½ cup skim milk
1 tablespoon oat bran
1 teaspoon pure vanilla extract
Pinch nutmeg
6 pecan halves
1 teaspoon unsweetened coconut,
   shredded

Place yam cubes in 8-cup glass measure with orange juice concentrate and cinnamon stick. Cover with vented plastic wrap, and microwave on High for 4 to 6 minutes, until soft, rotating cup and stirring mid-cycle. Add remaining ingredients, except pecans and coconut, and microwave covered on High for 2 more minutes.

(Please turn page)

Turn into blender or food processor and whip until smooth. Serve warm (or chill in freezer for 1 hour) in dessert dishes, topped with pecans and sprinkling of coconut.

· **Serves:** 4
· **Cooking time:** 6 to 8 minutes
· **Preparation time:** 10 minutes
· **Per Serving:** 5 Chol (mg);   22 Carbo (g);   3 Prot (g);
   20 Na (mg)
   Dietary Fiber: 2.1g
   Fat (g): 2; Sat .4; Poly .5; Mono 1.1
   Calories: 109
   Exchanges: 1 starch/bread; ½ fruit

Jane's Red Applesauce

3 Golden Delicious apples, cut into
   eighths
½ cup fresh cranberries
1 tablespoon frozen orange juice
   concentrate
1 cinnamon stick
4 pecan halves

Place all ingredients, except pecans, in a 1-quart measure and cover with well-vented plastic wrap. Microwave on High for 3 minutes. Stir, and microwave on High another 2 to 3 minutes, until apples are soft. Discard cinnamon stick, turn into a food mill, and grind over a bowl. Chill until ready to serve, and top with a few pecans.

· **Serves:** 4
· **Cooking time:** 5 to 6 minutes
· **Preparation time:** 10 minutes plus chilling time
· **Per Serving:** 0 Chol (mg);   18 Carbo (g);   1 Prot (g);
    0 Na (mg)
    Dietary Fiber: 2.6g
    Fat (g):   2;   Sat .2;   Poly .5;   Mono 1.1
    Calories: 86
    Exchanges: 1 fruit

Orange Cheese Cake

1 cup part-skim ricotta cheese
¼ cup 1% cottage cheese
2 eggs, 1 yolk only
1 tablespoon pure vanilla extract
1 teaspoon maple extract
Pinch nutmeg
1 tablespoon whole wheat pastry flour
2 tablespoons frozen orange juice
   concentrate
3 tablespoons orange peel, grated
4 tablespoons Grapenuts
4 sliced strawberries, blueberries, kiwi,
   or banana for topping if desired

In a deep bowl, combine first nine ingredients, reserving 1 tablespoon of orange peel. Beat with a hand mixer or use food processor to blend quickly. Turn into a 9-inch quiche or pie dish, and microwave at 80% power for 8 minutes, rotating the dish once. Microwave on High for 2 minutes more. Cake is baked when a knife inserted in center comes out clean.

Dust top with Grapenuts and reserved orange peel. Refrigerate for a few hours, or make this the day prior to serving. Before serving, top with sliced fruit or berries. Lemon juice and lemon rind may be substituted for the orange.

· **Serves:** 6
· **Cooking time:** 10 minutes
· **Preparation time:** 15 minutes plus chilling time
· **Per Serving:** 57 Chol (mg);   10 Carbo (g);   8 Prot (g);
     97 Na (mg)
     Dietary Fiber: .7g
     Fat (g):   4;   Sat 2.0;   Poly .2;   Mono 1.2
     Calories: 101
     Exchanges: 1 skim milk;   ½ fat

Pink Pear Poach

. . . .

2 ripe Anjou pears, pared and
quartered
¼ cup orange juice
1 slice lemon
1 tablespoon unsweetened cran-
berry juice
Dash each of powdered cinnamon
and ginger
Few whole cloves
2 to 3 large ripe strawberries, sliced
1 teaspoon almonds, slivered

Arrange pears in one layer in round 9-inch glass pie
plate. Add all ingredients, except almonds, and
cover with wax paper. Microwave on High 2
minutes. Turn, recover, and microwave on High another 2 minutes. Uncover, discard cloves, and garnish with almonds when ready to serve, warm or
chilled.

· Serves: 4
· Cooking time: 4 minutes
· Preparation time: 7 minutes
· Per Serving: 0 Chol (mg);   16 Carbo (g);   1 Prot (g);
        0 Na (mg)
    Dietary Fiber: 2.9g
    Fat (g):   1;   Sat .1;   Poly .2;   Mono .3
    Calories: 66
    Exchanges: 1 fruit

Note: other fruits such as oranges, kiwis, or berries may be substituted for pineapple tidbits and apples.

· **Serves:** 4
· **Cooking time:** 8 to 9 minutes
· **Preparation time:** 15 minutes
· **Per Serving:** 0 Chol (mg);   37 Carbo (g);   2 Prot (g);
    26 Na (mg)
    Dietary Fiber: 4.3g
    Fat (g): 1; Sat .5; Poly .2; Mono .4
    Calories: 153
    Exchanges: 1½ starch/bread; 1 fruit

Index

A

Good Health Books from Surrey

The Free and Equal® Cookbook by Carole Kruppa
From appetizers to desserts, these 150-plus, *sugar-free* recipes will make your mouth water and your family ask for more! Make great dishes like cioppino, Caesar salad, shrimp Louisiana, stuffed peppers, and chicken cacciatore, yet keep control of calories, cholesterol, fat, and sodium. Calorie counts and diabetic exchanges.

The Free and Equal® Dessert Cookbook by Carole Kruppa
Make cheesecake, black bottom pie, chocolate bon bons, cookies, cakes—in all, 160 *sugar-free* desserts. Calorie counts and diabetic exchanges.

Skinny Soups by Ruth Glick and Nancy Baggett
More than 100 delicious, hearty, calorie-wise soups from elegant crab and mushroom bisque to exotic Malaysian chicken scallion to chilled soups and standbys such as French onion, chicken-rice, and New England fish chowder. Recipes keep careful control of fat, sodium, and cholesterol. Complete nutritional data.

The Microwave Diabetes Cookbook by Betty Marks
More than 130 delicious, time-saving *sugar-free* recipes for everyone concerned with heart-health, and especially those with diabetes. Everything from appetizers to desserts, vichyssoise to pizza. Complete nutritional data and diabetic exchanges.

Thinner Dinners in Half the Time by Carole Kruppa
Make your own diet dishes—such as Mediterranean artichoke dip, roast pork chops Calypso, chicken Veronique, and marinated salmon with pasta—then freeze ahead to keep your fridge filled with fast fixings. Over 160 delicious time-savers.

The Restaurant Companion: A Guide to Healthier Eating Out
by Hope Warshaw, M.M.Sc., R.D.
All the practical information you need to order low-cal, low-fat, high-nutrition meals in 15 popular cuisines! Includes ethnic restaurants, fast-food chains, even airlines.

Skinny Spices by Erica Levy Klein
50 nifty homemade spice blends, ranging from Ha Cha chili to Moroccan mint, to make even diet meals exciting! Spice blends require no cooking and add *zero* fat, cholesterol, or calories to food. Includes 100 recipes.

The Love Your Heart Low Cholesterol Cookbook by Carole Kruppa
250 low-cholesterol recipes for everything from appetizers to desserts. Enjoy the great tastes—with *no* cholesterol—of deviled eggs, Italian bean soup, oriental chicken salad, chocolate cake, and many more easy-to-make delights. Complete nutritional data.

Feeding Your Baby: From Conception to Age 2 by Louise Lambert-Lagacé
First U.S. edition. Complete information on good nutrition for babies—and mothers—before, during, and after pregnancy. Includes breast-feeding (with tips for working moms), advice on formulas, how to introduce solids, recipes for homemade baby foods, dealing with problem eaters, and much more.